MW00608481

PTARMIGAN TELEGRAPH

GREG ASIMAKOUPOULOS

PTARMIGAN
TELEGRAPH

THE STORY OF RADIO STATION KICY

To Mark & Patty
Thanks for allowing me
to stay at your beautiful
home & preach in your
delightful church.
Enjoy this
True Alaska tale!

ARCTIC BROADCASTING ASSOCIATION, INC.
CHICAGO, ILLINOIS

Arctic Broadcasting Association, Inc.
5101 N. Francisco Avenue
Chicago, IL 60625
www.kicy.org

© 2004 by Arctic Broadcasting Association, Inc.

All rights reserved.

Scripture taken from the Holy Bible, New International Version. Copyright © 1973, 1978, 1984 International Bible Society.

Cover art: "Ptarmigan Telegraph" by Rie Muñoz, Juneau, Alaska, © 1976 Rie Muñoz Ltd. www.riemunoz.com

Cover and book design: Steven Luce

ISBN 0-9755150-0-4

Printed in the United States of America

14 13 12 11 10 09 08 07 06 05 04 1 2 3 4 5 6 7 8 9 10

To those who have served KICY as paid staff, volunteers, and supporters.

Always give yourselves fully to the work of the Lord, because you know that your labor in the Lord is not in vain.
                                                                    —*1 Corinthians 15:58, NIV*

CONTENTS

FOREWORD

The author's analogy between the history of KICY and the Iditarod Trail Sled Dog Race is keenly astute. The Iditarod embodies the spirit of the 1925 serum run that brought much needed medicine to the children of Nome to keep them alive during the terrible diphtheria epidemic that winter. When there seemed to be no possible way to get the medicine to Nome, a brave and selfless group of men and dogs challenged all odds and delivered the serum. Many lives were saved. Likewise, the creation of KICY and its continued growth have kept the spirit and souls of its listeners alive for many years.

Growing up in Nome during the time when the only radio station was the Armed Services station, which was aired late at night, I remember KICY coming on air as a huge event in the community. It is hard for people to imagine the isolation that accompanied living in Nome. Our connections to the world outside of Nome were limited. There was no television or roads connecting us to other communities. Even our groceries had to be delivered on one of the three barges that came from Seattle during the summer months before the ocean froze solid. You had better have ordered enough groceries to last for the year, or you might go hungry! KICY helped us to feel more connected to those in our community and to the world.

Our growing-up years were closely tied to the Covenant Church. My mother, Lois McIver, was a daughter of pioneer Alaska missionaries L.E. and Ruth Ost. My parents and my two aunts raised their families in Nome. Between us, there were twenty grandchildren, so the Ost family was a major presence in the Nome Covenant Church. Beyond our strong family connection, KICY also tied us to the Covenant Church.

I will never forget Gert Fondell's "Lines from a Mother's Scrapbook," or one particular song that played so often, I never wanted to hear it again! The name of the song was "Little White Duck" and for one whole year it seemed that it was the only song on the request line. Needless to say, this wasn't what we young teenagers wanted to listen to.

One of the truly wonderful services KICY has offered from the beginning is the "Ptarmigan Telegraph." People throughout the northland have depended on this simple program that allows people to send personal messages over the airwaves. It has tied families together by providing critical instruction, services, and information. When our family went mining in the Council area, "Ptarmigan Telegraph" provided a vital service for us to get supplies and messages to our family in Nome that we were fine. Many folks have depended on this unique form of communication over the decades.

It is so important that this part of Alaska's history be saved. Future generations can look back at the struggles and heartbreaks that occurred in trying to get KICY on air and they will understand the great importance of God's mission for the northern Arctic hemisphere.

GAIL PHILLIPS
Former Speaker of the Alaska State House of Representatives

PREFACE

For almost forty-five years radio station KICY in Nome, Alaska, has been an important means of connecting the lives of the people who live in western Alaska. One of its most popular programs is called "Ptarmigan Telegraph," which allows people to send personal messages over the airwaves. In most areas, the use of public airwaves for personal communication is prohibited by the Federal Communications Commission, but the FCC allows it in rural Alaska, where many villages are isolated and the only means of travel from village to village is by plane or dog sled. The cover art provided by celebrated Alaskan artist Rie Muñoz graphically depicts how important "Ptarmigan Telegraph" is to those who live in western Alaska.

Until *Ptarmigan Telegraph: The Story of Radio Station KICY* was written there was no connection between the many stories written about KICY and the oral histories of those who helped to start the station. Arctic Broadcasting Association, an affiliated corporation of the Evangelical Covenant Church and owner and operator of KICY, hopes that by commissioning *Ptarmigan Telegraph* we have provided the connection, ensuring that the history of KICY is captured while those who lived it are still with us. The stories of those who had the vision for this pioneer work are truly remarkable and point us to a God who is faithful and who worked many miracles to see KICY reach its goal of spreading the gospel to western Alaska and the Russian Far East.

Clearly, the story of KICY involves the efforts of many of God's faithful servants and it could not be told without highlighting those who played a large role in the station's founding and operation. While we like to mention everyone who played a role in the ministry of KICY, we ultimately felt that the work flowed better if we focused on the story and its key players. This is not to diminish the role of the over 500 people who served as volunteers at some time with KICY. We have listed those folks in the appendix as way of honoring those whose gifts have enriched the ministry.

When writing a historical account, it is inevitable that we wrestle with terms and phrases that have changed over time. Those of you who are familiar with the history of the Evangelical Covenant Church's mission work in Alaska may notice that the names of some individuals, such as Uyabak, Axel Karlson's first convert, are spelled differently than in other Covenant sources. It is important to note the Iñupiaq language was not a formal written language until the mid-sixties, when Roy Ahmaogak, an ordained Presbyterian minister, translated the New Testament into Iñupiaq. Prior to this it was strictly a verbal language and there were no standards to its spelling. For this book, we have used the on-line Iñupiaq Dictionary developed by the University of Alaska's Institute of Social and Economic Research.

When it was possible to do so without changing the historical record, terms and phrases have been updated to reflect current sensitivities. The most notable example is the use of the term "Alaska Native" in place of "Eskimo." For those accustomed to the term "Native American," the use of Alaska Native may seem strange, but it is the term commonly used and preferred in Alaska.

A work of this magnitude could not have become a reality without the help of many people. The author and Arctic Broadcasting Association would like to thank Ralph Hanson, Bill Hartman, Ralph and Gert Fondell, Roald Amundsen, Fred Savok, Mina Bachelder, Ernie Hansen, Dave and Mitzi Shinen, Jim Engwall, Chip Swanson, Dave and Kathy DeVries, Terry Reynolds, Maggie Olson, Ted Haney, John McBride, Dave Oseland, Dennis

Weidler, Deanna Nelson, Curtis Ivanoff, Patty Burchell, Frances Whitmore, Harvey Fiskeaux, Robert C. Larson, Steve Dawson, Rob Hall, Margaret Zylstra Davidson, Len Zylstra, Jonathan Zylstra, Cathy (Zylstra) Owens, Phil Anderson, Jim Bruckner, and Ernest Owen for their contributions to the manuscript.

We are grateful to Rie Muñoz and Juan Muñoz of Rie Muñoz Ltd. for allowing us to use Rie's 1976 image "Ptarmigan Telegraph" for our cover art.

We also want to thank Ellen Engseth of the Covenant Archives for her assistance in locating primary sources and helping with fact checking. The Evangelical Covenant Church's Department of Communication is also owed a debt of gratitude for their assistance with this project. In particular, we want to thank Evy Lennard for reviewing and fact checking the manuscript and Steve Luce for the cover and book design. Last, but not least, Jane Swanson-Nystrom, managing editor of publications for the Covenant, is owed a heartfelt thank you for her guidance and encouragement throughout the process. Her skill and experience as an editor were invaluable to us as we sought to accurately tell the story of KICY.

When this project was first proposed we knew that getting the right author was critical. We needed someone who would respect the history and make the story come alive. Greg Asimakoupoulos served at KICY in 1987 as a volunteer in our time of need and he again answered our call for help by agreeing to take on the daunting challenge of connecting the various stories into a cohesive telling of the history of KICY. We appreciate his dedication in seeing this project through to completion.

Finally we want to thank all those who had the vision for KICY and most importantly we want to acknowledge God's faithfulness to KICY in these many years. We earnestly hope that this telling of the history of KICY will bring glory and honor to God.

ARCTIC BROADCASTING ASSOCIATION
Chicago, Illinois

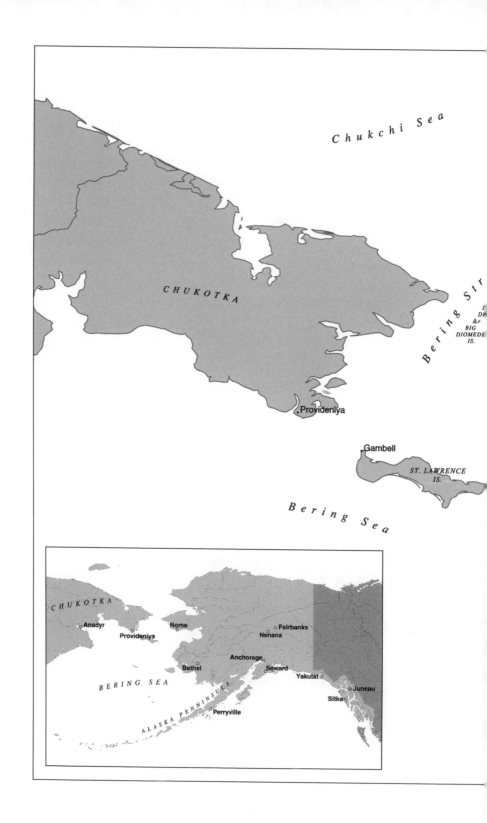

The Voice of the Arctic
by
Greg Asimakoupoulos

In the wilderness a voice is heard
declaring the word of the Lord.
It's not Elijah who's speaking
(or even the Baptist named John).
Far from it.
In fact, this voice is far from most.
It's the 50,000 watt voice
beaming from the coast of western Alaska
to the shores of eastern Siberia
and the windswept villages in between.
It's "The Voice of the Arctic"
calling the land of the midnight sun
to the One who alone
can fill the darkest heart
with the brilliant Light of day.

INTRODUCTION

The setting sun casts an orange glow on the Bering Sea. Here the ocean is frozen, and the reflection is eerily surreal. In the distance a parka-clad musher and his team of dogs move in the direction of the disappearing orb. A continuous wind whips the snow from the treeless tundra southward to the sea. The musher urges his team forward—they are only four miles from their goal.

A large crowd has assembled near the burled arch on Front Street in Nome, Alaska. Townsfolk and tourists excitedly await the arrival of the dog team and driver. The town of 3,500 has temporarily grown by a third. It happens every March when the Iditarod Trail Sled Dog Race culminates here. It's a far cry from the 20,000 gold-seekers and merchants that called Nome home in 1901. Still, several hundred warm bodies on the ice-covered streets is a remarkable sight.

The perspective that the bush pilots have from 5,000 feet in the air is also impressive. As the Iditarod "air force" flies dog food in and injured animals out, they see the miles that separate the sixty-some mushers and dog teams on the trail. While some are sleeping, others trudge on over snow and ice in hopes of improving their advantage before taking a break.

The Iditarod is a grueling trail of 1,100 miles from Anchorage to Nome

3

that is fraught with blinding blizzards, sub-zero temperatures, and diverse terrain. The trail takes anywhere from nine to twenty-nine days to complete. The courageous competitors and their canine teams believe in what they are doing. They are committed to a goal. It's not just the cash prizes for crossing the finish line. It's the pride that comes with doing what few will ever do.

In 1973, Joe Reddington Sr., an Anchorage businessman, and Howard Farley, a Nome meat-cutter and president of the Nome Kennel Club, devised a way to preserve the disappearing art of dog mushing. The Iditarod—known as the "Last Great Race"—has achieved its purpose, paying homage to a mode of transportation that for generations connected villages that were isolated by severe weather and vast distance. In addition to the Iditarod, the Junior Iditarod, the Yukon Quest, and the Junior Yukon Quest annually provide adults and youth with an opportunity to test their endurance and skill on dog trails. While dog teams and their mushers appeared to be a vanishing breed a generation ago, that is far from the case today.

Crowds line Front Street as a musher approaches the finish line of the Iditarod.

Although Nome was at one time synonymous with the gold rush, that is no longer true today. Now when Nome is mentioned in the news outside Alaska, chances are it is in relationship to the men and women who mush their dogs there. The Iditarod Trail Sled Dog Race and its related tourism has become Nome's new gold mine.

For those associated with a small denomination known as the Evangelical Covenant Church, the mention of Nome might also conjure up thoughts of a radio station. Since Easter Sunday 1960, KICY has broadcast entertaining, informative, and inspirational programming for residents of Nome, the outlying villages, and for those in Russia who can pick up the station's directional signal.

The story of how KICY came into being is a fascinating one. So are the goals this remarkable station has achieved as it approaches its fiftieth anniversary. The incredible journey that has led to its current ministry is not unlike that of a thousand-mile sled dog race. There have been obstacles, storms, weary participants, and an overarching goal that has kept the dream alive. And like the mushers and their dog teams, KICY has provided the remote towns and villages of the Seward Peninsula a connection with each other and the broader world. A daunting mission, which at times seemed impossible, has by the grace of God and the determination of visionary leaders become a reality. This is their story.

In Search of a Back Door to Russia

On Monday afternoon, March 10, 2003, Robert Sørlie pulled into the Iñupiaq village of Unalakleet, the largest (pop. 800) of the towns between Anchorage, the start of the Iditarod Trail, and Nome, where the race ends. Sørlie, a forty-five-year-old fire fighter from Norway, knew he was leading the pack of mushers, but he wasn't sure by how much. He soon found out. Within seventy minutes of Sørlie's arrival, Ramy Brooks and his dog team reached the town. Because of its position on the Bering Sea, Unalakleet marks the end of the sheltered trail. From here on harsh winds and unpredictable weather makes the dash to Nome a daring feat.

Although Brooks overtook Sørlie in the town of Elim en route to Nome, he was not able to maintain the lead. By midnight on March 13, approaching Nome, Sørlie was two hours ahead of Brooks. By two in the morning, a crowd of 1,000 enthusiastic Iditarod fans had gathered on Front Street in Nome. Ignoring the sub-zero temperature and a brisk northerly breeze, these diehard faithful cheered the Norwegian as he drove his team of dogs across the finish line.

Of the sixty-four competitors who had begun the Iditarod nine days earlier, Robert Sørlie was the first to glide beneath the famous burled wood arch. With only eight of the sixteen dogs with which he had begun the *thousand-mile trek, a virtual unknown became the first Scandinavian to win the Iditarod.*

The story of radio station KICY in Nome, Alaska, begins with the saga of Axel Karlson, a young minister of the Mission Covenant Church of Sweden. Although he would not live long enough to listen to a radio (let alone understand how important it would become to the communities in western Alaska), he laid the foundation for the station's development.

As a young man, Karlson felt a strong call to commit his life to ministry. He wanted to bring the message of salvation in Christ to those who had not heard the gospel story. In 1880 the Mission Covenant Church of Sweden commissioned Karlson as an evangelist and sent him east into Russia. Heading to Archangel in the northernmost part of Russia, Karlson set out to witness to Swedish sailors. He also planned to learn the language of the nomadic Samogitians in order to share Christ with them.

But Karlson faced opposition from the Russian Orthodox Church and the czarist government. He was arrested and jailed in the Central Moscow Prison and the authorities planned to send him to Siberia as a political prisoner. The Swedish State Department intervened, and in 1885 Karlson was released and allowed to return to Sweden.

Although grateful that God had answered the prayers of those who interceded on his behalf, Karlson was not content to stay home. The young missionary's sense of call was bolstered by something he had heard attributed to Swedish explorer Nils Adolf Erik Nordenskiold, who had encountered Alaska Natives while navigating the Bering Straits en route to the North Pole in 1879. Upon returning to Sweden, Baron Nordenskiold confided to E.J. Ekman, president of the Mission Covenant Church of Sweden, that there were native tribes in Siberia and Alaska who needed to hear the gospel.

When Karlson heard Ekman quote Nordenskiold, he offered to go. A fellow Covenanter by the name of Adolph Lydell expressed a similar interest. He had spent the previous few years in Russia evangelizing the Swedish workers at the invitation of Alfred Nobel who operated petroleum plants in Baku. Lydell had left Russia when his wife had become ill and eventually died.

Both Karlson and Lydell were ready to accept a new challenge and lose themselves in it. In 1886 the Swedish Covenant Church called the two men to minister in the Russian Arctic. Even though Karlson had been spared Siberian exile, he was willing to go there as a missionary. This time, however, he would travel to Russia by going west.

The two arrived in New York and made their way to Chicago. While waiting for their westbound connections, Karlson and Lydell met with transplanted Swedes who were part of the American Mission Covenant Church, which had organized officially the year before. En route to San Francisco, they stopped in Rockford, Illinois, to attend the second annual meeting of the young denomination. While there the two were given an opportunity to describe their plans with gathered delegates.

By the time the two Swedes arrived in San Francisco, the last northbound ship of the season had already left. They would have to spend the winter in California. Making the most of their unexpected layover, they preached to Scandinavian immigrants and attempted to learn English. During their time in California, they heard talk of an immediate need in Alaska for missionaries.

Alaska in 1887 was largely an unknown land. Only twenty years earlier the United States had purchased the Alaska Territory from the czar of Russia for $7,200,000. Although critics called the purchase "Seward's folly" after the secretary of state who negotiated the deal, acquiring a land mass more than twice the size of Texas—586,400 square miles—for 2.5 cents an acre was no small accomplishment.

Karlson wrote to the mission board in Sweden requesting that he and Lydell be allowed to focus their attention on Alaska instead of Siberia. His request was granted, and in the spring of 1887 they booked passage on a ship to Alaska.

When the captain of the ship discovered what Karlson and Lydell were planning to do, he attempted to dissuade them. "Don't you know that Eskimos have no souls? It is useless to preach to them!" he protested. But the young missionaries had an overwhelming confidence that they were in the center of God's will.

As the ship drew nearer to Alaska, Karlson looked to God for guidance about where he should begin his ministry. His experience had taught him that God would make it clear in his perfect timing. An Episcopal missionary on board by the name of John Chapman proved to be the means by which God answered Karlson's prayer for guidance. He encouraged him to go north of the mouth of the Yukon River.

On June 25, 1887, Karlson disembarked at the village of St. Michael. He had said good-bye earlier to Lydell, who had decided to focus on a group of Indians know as Tlingit further south on the Yakutat Peninsula. Although Karlson was apprehensive about setting out into an unfamiliar territory, he knew God was leading him.

Karlson met a Russian-speaking native who was the Iñupiaq chief from Unalakleet, a small village on the Bering Sea. Nashalook befriended Karlson and encouraged him to go with him to his village. Karlson agreed, and as they journeyed by foot to the village, he practiced saying "Unalakleet," which means where the east wind blows. In spite of twenty hours of daylight, which allowed for long days of travel, the trip was difficult and took two weeks to complete.

Life in the village did not begin smoothly for the hopeful missionary. Some men threatened to kill him and for three months Karlson had to live under the chief's protection. Finally, when the danger had passed, he built his own quarters and was able to visit several villages during his first winter there.

Karlson befriended a teenage boy named Uyabak (Iñupiaq for "rock") who was orphaned when his father was murdered while traveling to St. Michael. Karlson taught him English and employed him to be his interpreter and sled dog driver. As trust developed between the two, Uyabak opened his heart to the missionary's message and became Karlson's first convert.

The severe weather and the isolation of a winter in Alaska took their toll on Karlson. He wrote in his diary of bouts with loneliness and rheumatism. After his first year there, Karlson chose to make a trip back to the United States for supplies.

While traveling, Karlson was informed that the Swedish denomination had entered into conversations with the American Covenant to have them take over the oversight of Karlson and the Alaska project. And so in 1889 the Evangelical Mission Covenant Church of America had its first missionary in its first mission field. When Karlson returned to Alaska, he was accompanied by August Anderson, a missionary who had been assigned to work with him by the Swedish church before the transfer of responsibility had been made official.

By the fall of 1889, Karlson, with the company of his Swedish-speaking colleague, was beginning to feel accepted. Unfortunately, the Iñupiaqs were not as willing to accept his message of the gospel. Although Uyabak, who became known as Rock, had been willing to trust Christ, his response did not reflect the majority in Unalakleet.

Uyabak

Karlson recognized that his primary task was to win friends before attempting to win converts. He used his knowledge in carpentry to help adults in the village construct homes. In the process, he laid foundations for both dwellings and relationships.

He also began a school for children. He wanted to teach them how to read and write. The children of the village responded warmly to the man with wire-rimmed glasses. They called him Isregalik, "the man with the glass eyes." Using the Bible as a textbook for teaching English, Karlson explained the message of God's love while introducing the children to words that sounded strange to them. In his journal in 1889 Karlson made the following entry on the day classes began: "Today in the Lord's name we began school for the children. Twenty-nine children were present, twenty boys and nine girls. The children all got new names and some clean clothes and promised to wash their faces each morning."

In spite of the difficulty winning converts, news of Karlson's work in Unalakleet resulted in a growing surge of excitement among Covenant churches. By 1891, the church sent five additional missionaries to Alaska— David Johnson, Hanna Swenson, Agnes Wallin, Agnes Carlson, and Selma

Peterson. The church also purchased a boat and a small sawmill for the mission. With the additional personnel and equipment, Karlson was able to construct a children's home in Unalakeet. Hanna Swenson oversaw the operation of the home. Soon after she arrived, Swenson and Karlson were married.

The following year, Karlson traveled to the Covenant Annual Meeting in Rockford, Illinois, where he inspired delegates with the potential of the work in Alaska. They generously opened their wallets, allowing Karlson to return with nearly $2,000 and renewed determination. That zeal resulted in mission extensions in Golovin and Shaktoolik.

Axel and Hanna Karlson

By the early 1890s, Karlson's investment in friendship evangelism was beginning to pay off. Alaska Natives in and around Unalakleet were coming to faith. Among the first converts were Frank Kamaroff, Stephan Ivanoff, and Andrew Kakorin. These men used their dog teams to travel as evangelists and encouragers from village to village throughout the Seward Peninsula. Operating a lending library of Christian literature, they transported books, Bibles, and pamphlets. Alice Omegichuak and a women named Kooleeruk bore witness to the power of the gospel among women.

In those first years, the growing mission was faced by a number of obstacles—geographical, cultural, and economic. Citing the journal entries of early missionaries, Karl Olsson in his book *By One Spirit* paints a somber picture of the harsh realities that confronted them: "It is a heroic record of battles with a capricious and cruel Nature as well as with her Arctic concomitants: loneliness, depression, and anxiety."

The influence of the Russian Orthodox Church was a challenge to the young mission. Even though Alaskans in general had not embraced this branch of Christianity, the historical Russian presence had influenced their thinking. When Karlson and his colleagues attempted to follow up new converts with baptism, the officials of the Russian church questioned the meaning that Covenanters ascribed to the sacrament.

Another challenge the missionaries encountered was the co-habitation practices of the Alaska Natives. Women were viewed as little more than second-class citizens. Iñupiaq men often had several wives to help them eek out a living on the stingy tundra.

But the greatest threat the growing mission faced began in 1893 when support for the growing mission was threatened as the American economy suffered a major depression. For three years giving from churches fell off significantly. Fortunately, a government program allowed the missionary schools to collect federal funding for each village child enrolled. This was a welcomed policy. So was the means by which reindeer from Lapland were imported to the Seward Peninsula for the sake of generating revenue. But finances were still tight.

Then in the late 1890s, gold was discovered on the Seward Peninsula, and soon the gold rush in Nome began. In a phenomenon that almost defies reason, the windswept town of Nome grew from 200 to 20,000 as fortune seekers flocked to Norton Sound to stake claims. With the prospectors and prosperity came brothels and bars. Even the notorious gunslinger Wyatt Earp opened a saloon on the town's Front Street to capitalize on the boom-town economy. What initially appeared to be good fortune was anything but.

Stephan
Ivanoff

13

Even some of the missionaries were caught up in the gold fever. The story of a certain claim at Anvil Creek outside of Nome is a saga of greed, avarice, deception, and litigation. In 1897, P. H. Anderson, a student from North Park College in Chicago, arrived in Golovin to work with N. O. Hultberg. He was soon exposed to the talk of the town. The next year he bought rights to the Number 9 Above claim at Anvil Creek for twenty dollars. It proved to be a financial bonanza. Over the next few years $385,000 worth of gold was mined from his claim.

But was the money his or the mission's? The question proceeded to sap the energy and focus from many who had come to Alaska to deny personal gain and seek God's kingdom. Anderson claimed the windfall was his. His colleagues thought otherwise. It was a battle that twice found its way to the United States Supreme Court and raged for twenty-two years until the U.S. Court of Appeals for the 8th Circuit finally dismissed it.

At the height of the gold rush in Nome, Axel and Hanna Karlson were on an extended furlough in the United States. By the time they returned in 1901, they found a mission field distracted by the gold rush.

Karlson recognized that a permanent church was needed in Unalakleet to take the place of the buildings they had used for worship in the previous fifteen years. The lack of available money didn't dissuade him. He built it with his own savings. In addition, he found ways to support the local people by creating jobs for them and generously remunerating them.

By the time Axel Karlson died in 1910, he had learned to communi-

Axel Karlson's grave marker in the cemetery in Unalakleet

cate in Iñupiaq and his faithfulness and integrity led the people to trust him and to listen to him. Because Karlson lived and preached faithfully, the Holy Spirit succeeded in making remarkable inroads for the kingdom of God.

"In 1890 there probably was not a single Christian Iñupiaq Eskimo," writes Ernest S. Burch Jr. in his essay, "The Iñupiat and the Christianization of Arctic Alaska." "Twenty years later, there was scarcely an Iñupiaq who was not a Christian." Those words are inscribed on Karlson's grave marker in Unalakleet. His impact was nothing short of remarkable.

Although Karlson never was able to return to Russia, his pioneer work among such villages as Unalakleet, Golovin, and Shaktoolik laid the foundation for a ministry that would, given the right circumstances and God's timing, successfully transmit the gospel message to the country in which he once was imprisoned—to a country he had been called to reach.

CHAPTER TWO

A Seed Is Planted

Long before the legendary Iditarod Trail Sled Dog Race was first run in 1973, a far more important race took place in Alaska. In January 1925, the lives of countless children in Nome were at stake. An epidemic of diphtheria broke out, and the town did not have a sufficient amount of antitoxin. Dr. Curtis Welch telegraphed Fairbanks, Anchorage, Seward, and Juneau, asking for help. Three hundred thousand units of serum were located at a hospital in Anchorage. It was the only supply in the entire state.

The problem was to get it to Nome in time to tide the epidemic. With the Bering Sea frozen and no railroad or roads extending to Nome's remote location, dog teams were the only solution. The 300,000 units were packed in a cylinder and wrapped in fur and canvas and transported to Nenana on an overnight train. The serum arrived at 11 p.m. on January 27. From there, it would be transported 674 miles by a sled dog relay race. It was a distance mushers who delivered the mail normally covered in a month. The dying children needed the medicine much sooner than that.

The first musher took the insulated cylinder fifty-two miles, and passed it on to the second musher who traveled thirty-one miles. From musher to musher the relay continued, involving a total of twenty sled dog drivers and their teams. The needed medicine arrived in Nome on February 2. It had taken only 127 hours for the lifesaving serum to arrive from Nenana due to the cooperative effort of individuals who braved sub-zero temperatures and blinding blizzards to save the children of Nome. Each year the Iditarod Trail Sled Dog Race commemorates that amazing feat.

The divided interests brought by the gold mining controversy, declining financial support from the denomination, and turnover of staff slowed the momentum of the early Alaska mission. The severe weather of the Seward Peninsula proved too extreme for many. So too the isolation from family and loved ones. But the passion to save souls did not dissipate. The early part of the twentieth century was marked by a series of missionaries who helped the mission maintain a forward motion, albeit slow.

O. P. Anderson, a Chicago pastor, resigned his church to travel to Alaska with the Good Hope Mining Company in hopes of striking it rich. However, once in Alaska, Anderson left the mining operation and joined the Golovin mission staff in 1900. For ten years he witnessed the power of God in remarkable ways. With his wife, Amanda, Anderson conducted Bible studies and introduced gospel music to the surrounding community. The results were amazing. Records indicate that Anderson baptized 447 people during his decade of ministry on the Norton Sound. Half of those were converted in 1903 alone.

Word of Anderson's ministry reached as far as Kotzebue, about 160 miles due north of Golovin, and in Shishmaref, about 140 miles northwest of Golovin. Traveling great distances by dog team, people came to hear Anderson preach. And as they traveled throughout the Seward Peninsula, the message of the gospel was beginning to link the villages of western Alaska.

Ludvig E. and Ruth Ost arrived in Golovin as the Andersons were leaving the mission. The Osts oversaw the mission outpost there, which included a children's home, a school, and a church. L. E. Ost's role as mission director also included the oversight of a growing reindeer population. Around the turn of the century, Presbyterian missionary and educator Sheldon Jackson had imported a herd from Siberia to provide the Alaska Natives income and a food source. The initial herd of some 1,200 grew exponentially. By 1917 the reindeer population in Alaska was 95,000 and peaked at 600,000 in 1936. Besides being used for food, the herds also were used to pull sleds, deliver mail, and transport people.

Soon after arriving in Golovin, Ost was managing more than 12,000 reindeer with the help of an overworked staff. The same occurred in Unalakleet where Henning Gustafson struggled to keep the mission together following Axel Karlson's death. It became obvious that raising reindeer was draining the energy away from propagating the gospel. Ironically, when the decision was made to disband the reindeer operation, the herds were growing, but the mission was not.

Tragically, in September 1913 the Golovin mission station was destroyed by a massive storm. Ost relocated his young family and a dozen Alaska Native children sixty miles by water further up the Norton Sound to a sheltered area of high hills and spruce trees. It was a heroic expedition that resulted in the establishment of a new village, which they called Elim.

Ludvig and Ruth Ost with Alaska Native children in Golovin

While the Osts attempted to build a mission outpost in Elim, the Gustafsons in Unalakleet were trying their best to rekindle a passion for evangelism and grow a healthy congregation that had been dispirited by the loss of Axel Karlson and his financial support. Meanwhile, financial troubles for the young Covenant denomination impacted the mission work in Alaska. In 1907 nearly $14,000 was earmarked for ministry to the Alaska Natives, but by 1913 the amount was a paltry $2,800. Despite the poor funding, by 1919 a new vision for ministry began to spread, resulting in renewed life for the Covenant's work in Alaska. Ost convinced the missions staff at Unalakleet (which by this time was under the direction of his brother-in-law Lars Almquist) to come to Elim for a meeting. Ost wanted them to pray for a strategy for future evangelism and church planting.

All the Alaska Native Christians were invited to the Elim conference held in the summer. Ost stood up before them and made a case of indigenous leadership. "By now you have been Christians long enough to know what is needed to carry on the work, and that you yourselves must support your own missionaries. We white people have come here to Alaska simply to help and support you. Now the time has come for you to take over a part of the responsibility."

The Alaskans welcomed the challenge. They gathered around Wilson Gonongnan from Golovin and, laying their hands on him in prayer, they consecrated him to full-time ministry. He became the first Alaska Native Covenant pastor. Within a few months, Wilson and his wife, Minnie, were laying a foundation for a new mission station in Mountain Village on the Yukon River.

Wilson Gonongnan (left), with two unidentified women

Two years after the Elim conference, Ost welcomed a visitor to Alaska who was determined to pick up where Axel Karlson had left off in trying to get into Russia by way of Siberia. Nils Hoijer, a sixty-four-year-old Swede, had spent twenty years in Russia as a missionary of the Covenant Church of Sweden. He now wanted to bring the gospel to a part of Russia that was not accessible from Scandinavia. Ost had met Hoijer while on a brief furlough in Chicago in 1917. At that time they had discussed Hoijer's interest in establishing a mission in the Russian Far East, and Ost extended an invitation to come to Alaska.

In 1921 Hoijer arrived in Alaska with C. J. Sodergren, a theologian and a leader in the Swedish Lutheran Church. Ost borrowed a schooner named *Jenny* and piloted the two would-be church planters up the Bering Strait to Little Diomede Island. With the help of two Alaska Natives as crew, the schooner sailed west to the eastern coast of Siberia. Excitement built as thoughts of reaching the isolated Russian people with the good news of Jesus were translated into more than wishful thinking as each mile passed. Not since David Johnson made a brief preaching mission in Siberia in 1896 (with Axel Karlson's first convert Rock at his side) had Covenant missionaries been able to enter Russia.

Within several days *Jenny* and her passengers were docked in Anadyr. Ost, Hoijer, and Sodergren announced their intentions to the officials there and waited for their request to be considered. To their amazement, they granted them permission to conduct missionary outreach. A certificate was issued allowing any or all of the men to stay in Anadyr or anywhere else on the Siberian coast.

The men returned to Alaska to prepare for an evangelistic outreach to Siberia. Although eager to begin the Russian mission, it took Hoijer two years to finalize his plans. He realized that he was too old to work full-time in Russia, so he recruited two missionaries from Alaska to join him. Anna Carlson and Ernst Andersson had worked at the mission in Elim and Unalakleet as a nurse and a teacher and were willing to expand the Covenant work in Russia.

In June 1923, just as the ice was breaking up in Norton Sound, L. E. Ost performed Ernst and Anna's wedding in Nome and then saw the couple off as they sailed westward with Hoijer. When they arrived at the coastal village of Naukon, Hoijer met with the Russian authorities while the newlyweds went to a guesthouse for lunch. There were two soldiers there as well. As they waited to be served, one of the soldiers reached for his rifle. To their horror, he shot and killed the other soldier. Shocked and frightened, the couple darted out of the little house and ran back down to the dock. They immediately returned to the Seward Peninsula and, within a year's time, they left the Alaska mission and moved to Minnesota to be near family.

For Hoijer the events surrounding the Anderssons' short-lived assignment was a devastating blow. Although he made several other visits to the Siberian coastal villages over the next couple years, he was not able to establish a permanent mission station there. Failing health and a subsequent shipwreck off the coast of Nome took its toll on the man who had attempted to rekindle Axel Karlson's dream. Nils Hoijer died in 1925.

Although plans of reaching Siberia were put on hold, the vision to extend the mission in Alaska was kept in focus. In 1926 a church was established in Hooper Bay with an Alaska Native pastor. In 1928 the Ost family left Elim and returned to Golovin. The expansive new home Ost built for his family was big enough to house the ministry of the mission, which after the devastating storm fifteen years earlier, was finally re-established.

Little by little churches were built and pastors called to village after village. These new infant fellowship groups included Mekoryuk on Nunivak Island, White Mountain, Candle, Solomon, Koyuk, and Bethel. Interestingly, the first three native pastors, Wilson Gonongnan, Misha Ivanoff, and Jacob Kenick were married to three sisters, Minnie, Alice, and Sara Omegichuak respectfully. But even beyond blood relations, there was a growing awareness of being God's family as congregations in these Alaska Native villages interacted with one another.

What was occurring in terms of spiritual planting and harvesting was also occurring in a much more literal sense at the oldest Covenant mission station. In 1923 the Covenant denomination sent a new pastor and mission director to Unalakleet. Ernst B. Larsson loved to garden. Not willing to accept the local wisdom that because of short summers and long winters, produce and flowers wouldn't grow, Larsson set out to prove otherwise. Starting with the small plot in back of the mission house, he

Ernst B.
Larsson

grew vegetables, fruit, and flowers that had never been seen at such a northern latitude.

Each summer as he expanded his garden, he was amazed at how large his cabbage, lettuce, and potatoes grew due to the twenty-plus hours of sunlight. He realized that gardening could be a means to supplement the operational budget of the mission and give the villagers food not only to eat but for use as barter for other needed staples. Gardens were planted throughout Unalakleet. Produce was harvested and regularly transported to Nome to be sold at the market. Large orders came from all across the state.

Vegetables grown by the Covenant mission in Unalakleet

Government officials came from Juneau, Anchorage, and Fairbanks to look at the gardens for themselves. The introverted Larsson gained the reputation as the "gardening pastor." Amazingly, this often-overlooked Covenant missionary is the genius behind a major agricultural phenomenon in Alaska's Matanuska Valley that encircles Anchorage.

Larsson's overriding passion however, was planting seeds of faith in the hearts of Alaska Native youth and adults. In addition to preaching and pastoral care, each year he created a twelve-week Bible school, offering courses in Bible, church history, English, and music. As he traveled up the coast of the Seward Peninsula, he hoped to reach beyond the Bering Sea. Aware of the original passion that had motivated Axel Karlson, Larsson wrote, "We pray, also, that the day may come when we may have the privilege and joy of sending the gospel to the Siberian natives for whom this mission was first intended."

In 1935, a young American pastor who would be directly involved in starting KICY, arrived in Golovin with his wife. Ralph and Alyce Hanson were assigned to provide pastoral leadership in both Golovin and White Mountain. As one who had come to appreciate the capability (and porta-bility) of radio, Hanson brought with him the best battery-operated receiv-er he could buy. He had hoped that a radio would help them feel more connected to the broader world, and less isolated. The nearest radio sta-tions, however, were 500 miles (by air) away in Anchorage and Fairbanks. The uneven topography of the mountainous wilderness that separated him from the transmitter towers resulted in a scratchy signal that would last for only a few minutes and then fade away.

Ralph and Alyce Hanson

Like the missionaries before him, one of the challenges Hanson faced was the difficulty of traveling between the villages. Although Golovin and White Mountain were only twenty-five miles apart, there were no roads connecting them (there were no cars) and it took four hours by dog sled. Hanson did not own a team and had to rent one to travel back and forth between his two churches. Bush planes were available by that time, but they were substantially more expensive.

One day while watching a small plane take off, Hanson had a thought. Why wouldn't it be possible to use an airplane engine to propel a sled across the frozen tundra? He could picture it. A couple pair of skis, a cus-tomized sleigh, and a gas-powered propeller was all he would need. As he shared his brainstorm with Alyce, she affirmed his ingenuity but gen-tly reminded him of the obvious. Where would he find an airplane engine? They were hundreds of miles from a supplier of airplane parts.

Hanson brought his concerns to God. He specifically asked for an air-plane engine. Not long after, he was visiting a friend. As he prepared to leave, Hanson looked over his friend's shoulder, and just to the side of the front door he saw an airplane engine. He had found an answer to his prayer in the last place he would have expected to find it. His friend was willing to sell the engine for twenty-five dollars.

Hanson assembled the four-speed Harley Davidson engine to a home-made passenger cabin and called his creation an airsled. It looked like a sawed-off airplane on skis with the propeller at the back. But it worked. And it saved time. The twenty-five-mile trek between Golovin and White Mountain could be completed in just under an hour. This precursor of the snowmobile (known as a snow machine in Alaska) also allowed Hanson to reach the surrounding villages of Council, Elim, and Bluff. He was able to travel the seventy miles to Nome, where both of his sons were born, in just one day.

Ralph Hanson in his homemade snow machine

In 1941 Alyce Hanson became ill and required medical attention that doctors in the area could not provide. After only six years, the Hansons had to return to the States. But Ralph's love for and commitment to Alaska would continue throughout his ministry, and his concern for improving access and communication between churches and villages would help create the vision for a radio ministry.

After serving as interim pastor of the Berkeley Covenant Church near San Francisco, where Alyce recovered, Ralph was called to become the denomination's secretary of missions. As such, Ralph Hanson would prove to play a pivotal role in the Covenant's decision to incorporate radio broadcasting into the Covenant's ministry in western Alaska.

The Birth of an Idea

Novice observers of sled dog races have questioned whether the sport is humane. They wonder if subjecting dogs to grueling runs constitutes cruelty to animals. But ask any musher and they will tell you how much their dogs love to race. From their perspective, the sled-pulling pups are in their glory when they are running in sub-zero temperatures on a snow-covered path. These are no ordinary dogs. They are carefully bred to handle the necessary six- to seven-mile-per-hour run with ease.

Similarly, the uniformed observer might question how the sled dog drivers can run the Iditarod year after year. How can they challenge the bitter elements of frigid winds and blinding snowstorms to reach the famed burled-wood arch on Front Street in Nome? The answer lies in the title given to a book by Christian theologian and writer Eugene Peterson: it's "a long obedience in the same direction." They fix their eyes on a worthy goal and persevere. Eleven hundred miles are traveled a mile at a time by those who know where they want to go and refuse to give up until they have reached their destination.

Just prior to the departure of Ralph and Alyce Hanson, Paul and Nell Carlson arrived in Alaska to help connect the villages of the Covenant mission. In 1937 Carlson accompanied Gust E. Johnson, secretary of foreign missions from 1933 to 1944, on Johnson's tour of Alaska. Johnson became convinced that the work of the Alaska mission could be greatly improved if the missionaries had a plane to ease the burden of travel. In 1938 the Covenant purchased a Fairchild Model 24 airplane and shipped it to Nome. Carlson, who had taken pilot training at Municipal Airport in Chicago while studying at North Park Seminary, then became one of the world's first missionary pilots. The cost of the airplane was quickly recouped by the time and money that was saved on travel. To fly round trip from Candle to Mountain Village cost $55. The same trip by dogsled cost close to $400.

Paul and Nell Carlson

But the Carlsons' contribution was not limited to Paul's abilities as a pilot. They were gifted evangelists and helped in the ongoing construction projects within various villages. They also played a key role in laying the foundation for the Covenant's radio ministry in Alaska. In 1943, the Carlsons invited another missionary family to join them in Nome for the Christmas holidays. Emory and Ruth Lindgren had arrived from Iowa the previous year to serve the congregation in the remote village of Candle. They were delighted to accept the invitation.

Following dinner on Christmas Eve, the two families listened on the Carlsons' radio to news of World War II as broadcast over the new Armed Forces radio station located in Nome. Station WXLN had been mandated by the government as a way of helping the military in Alaska maintain communications. It was only 400 watts but it connected the area to the rest of the world.

Before the evening was over, the Carlsons and Lindgrens gathered around the upright piano to sing carols and hymns. The harmony of the home-style quartet gave Nell an idea. Perhaps the Armed Forces radio station would be interested in broadcasting live Christmas music.

Despite the initial skepticism of the other three, Nell decided to pursue her idea. She bundled up and headed out the door and down the street to city hall where the station was located. She walked into the upstairs studio and introduced herself. Then she asked the lone radio operator if he would be interested in fifteen minutes of live Christmas music. His reply delighted her: "Absolutely—but couldn't you come up with enough material to fill a half hour time slot?" Nell agreed and they set an air date for the day following Christmas.

In addition to reading the Christmas story, opening gifts, and sharing a holiday meal together, the Carlsons and Lindgrens made the most of the next day. They chose and rehearsed songs for their upcoming performance. On December 26, 1943, the Christmas special, produced and performed by two Covenant missionary couples, was broadcast. The thirty-minute program included Christmas carols in four-part harmony, Scripture readings, and devotional thoughts.

That broadcast was the first time the Christian message had been presented on radio throughout the Seward Peninsula and across the Norton Sound. The station received letters of gratitude from listeners in Golovin, White Mountain, Unalakleet, Teller, and Shishmaref. With the permission of the Armed Forces radio station, the Carlsons, Lindgrens, and several others from various villages continued to write and produce simple, weekly programs of Christian music and devotional messages.

Radio's influence was significant. During the long years of a bitter war, Franklin Roosevelt rallied the nation through his fireside chats, commu-

Emory and Ruth Lindgren

nicating with listeners as though they were in the same room. In the same way, the weekly religious programming on the Armed Forces station inspired Christians up and down the coast.

In 1945 Paul Carlson negotiated a network of shared ministry among the ministers in town, establishing the Nome Ministerial Association. He made sure that each pastor had a turn at the microphone for the devotional radio broadcasts. In addition, he succeeded in creating within the local pastors (and their congregations) an appetite for what radio could accomplish for the sake of the gospel. Under Paul's direction, the ministerial association took over the production of the weekly Christian radio programs.

Gust E. Johnson (left), secretary of missions, and G.F. Hedstrand, editor of the *Covenant Weekly*, pose with the denomination's first plane in Alaska.

The Armed Forces station provided only minimal spiritual content for Christians in villages along the Seward Peninsula. New believers required more than thirty minutes of programming granted each Sunday to the local churches. To that end Paul logged many miles in his plane flying to such places as White Mountain, Unalakleet, and Golovin, to provide pastoral care and biblical teaching.

As Paul's responsibilities as leader of the Covenant's Alaska mission and missionary pilot increased, another couple from the States arrived to join the growing team of Covenant missionaries. Roald and Harriet Amundsen took over the pastoral responsibilities at the Nome Covenant Church. They also welcomed the opportunity to give direction to the radio programs produced by the ministerial association. Seeking out those with creative ideas and willing voices, the Amundsens embraced a vision of reaching the surrounding villages with the gospel through radio.

This vision was also shared by Edgar Swanson, secretary of home missions for the Covenant, who visited Alaska in March 1945 to be the denominational representative at the annual missionary council meeting. After the meetings, Swanson visited some of the mission stations. He reported his findings to the denomination in a series of articles he wrote for the *Covenant Weekly*. It was Swanson's comments in the June 15, 1945, edition that proved prophetic: "Alaska affords a unique radio possibility for the territory and for the entire northern hemisphere. Some evangelical group should capitalize on it."

In response to Swanson's observations and the urging of the missionaries in Alaska, the Executive Board of the Covenant appointed a committee in 1945 to study the possibilities of launching a radio ministry in Alaska. That spring the Department of Foreign Missions designated that the annual Easter appeal go to Alaska missions, and referred to plans for a radio station. The appeal raised $4,679.75. The committee's report, however, was not encouraging and identified a number of obstacles that stood in the way of developing a radio ministry. The most significant obstacles were the lack of qualified personnel to staff a radio ministry and the high start-up costs. The topic was subsequently tabled and the money raised was disbursed to other existing radio ministries in the United States.

While churches in Nome were continuing their broadcasts on Armed Forces radio, a young American sailor, who had recently completed his training as an electronic technician's mate, was sensing God's call to ministry. Ralph Fondell, who was stationed in Tsingtao, China, in early 1946, observed the ravages of war and was moved by the physical and

Edgar
Swanson

spiritual poverty of the people. "When I attended a Youth for Christ rally in Tsingtao, I saw Christian Chinese young people who were quite different from the masses I saw on the street begging or involved in prostitution," he later recalled. "That really made a dramatic impact on me. I could sense the Lord prompting me to be part of a ministry that could introduce Chinese youth who'd never heard of Jesus to his life-changing power."

In March 1946, Ralph received orders to a base on the island of Guam to serve as a radio technician with the Joint Communication Agency. While there, he was hit by a military vehicle while walking on the side of the road. As he lay in a hospital bed recovering, Ralph contemplated what life as a missionary might mean.

Ralph had grown up on his family's farm in Dawson, Minnesota. As a boy he was fascinated with broadcasting, and would listen to the vacuum-tube radio in the family barn as he milked cows before and after school. A friend's family owned a cabinet radio, and Ralph would join them as they listened to such programs as "The Old Fashioned Revival Hour," "Back to the Bible," and the "All Night Prayer Meeting." The messages he heard warmed his heart, but the technology of radio captured his imagination. The invisible airwaves that transmitted voices and music for hundreds of miles seemed magical. Wanting to learn more, he signed up for a correspondence course in radio electronics.

When he was drafted by the Army in October 1944, he took the Eddy Aptitude Test, which identified candidates for electronics training. By taking the test he was automatically transferred to the Navy, and while at boot camp at the Great Lakes Naval Base he learned he had passed the test. He was then transferred to the radio technician boot camp. There he began an almost twelve-month training program to become an electronic technician's mate.

As his leg healed in Guam, Ralph wondered how he could pursue both his love for radio and his growing call to ministry. Would he have to give up one for the other? On the ship back to the States, Ralph felt peace as he contemplated Revelation 3:8: "I know your deeds. See, I have placed before you an open door that no one can shut. I know that you have little strength, yet you have kept my word and have not denied my name." Ralph found courage to believe that God would open and close doors in a future that still lacked clarity.

Back in Dawson, Ralph made plans to attend North Park College in Chicago. He discovered that the new pastor of his home church had a daughter at North Park. As they got acquainted at home and at school, Ralph Fondell and Gert Franklin realized how much they had in common. Each had a desire to serve God in a cross-cultural setting. The more Ralph shared stories of his experiences in China, the more willing Gert was to consider following God's leading to the Far East. But in 1948 the diplomatic doors to Mainland China were closed, and the Covenant Church's longtime mission there ended.

After marriage and additional schooling for Ralph at the University of Minnesota, the couple returned to Chicago where Ralph enrolled at North Park Seminary. While taking a course in missions, Ralph met the secretary of foreign missions. It was none other than the former Alaskan missionary Ralph Hanson.

The seminarian expressed his desire to somehow extend the boundaries of Christ's kingdom through missionary radio. Hanson, who in spite of the findings of the 1945 radio committee had not given up on his dream of a radio ministry in Alaska, informed Fondell that he believed if the Covenant ever decided to make the investment of dollars, facilities, and personnel that missionary radio would require, the location of such a radio ministry would likely be Alaska. Fondell could tell as he visited with Hanson how much his heart still beat for the Alaska Natives he had served for six years.

Hanson's suggestion was all the encouragement Fondell needed. Retreating to the seminary library, he wrote a ninety-three-page term paper about missions in Alaska. The concluding section of that paper he titled, "Why Not Radio in Alaska?" In it he outlined a rationale for why the Covenant should build a radio station. The more he researched his thesis, the more convinced he became that God was calling Gert and him to the northland.

Among other things in the lengthy treatise, Fondell wrote, "The competition in the field of radio broadcasting [in Alaska] appears to be almost nil; however, communications by shortwave radio are as popular in even the remote villages of Alaska as the party-line telephone in the rural United States. The natives in the remotest villages crave for contact with others.... The vast turnover of missionaries on the field regardless of the group, together with the tremendous task of even evangelizing a small community, seems to indicate that the occasional personal contact by the missionary is not the complete answer to most effective witnessing in Alaska...."

The plan to pursue a radio ministry seemed like a good fit. Ralph Fondell became convinced he wasn't cut out to be a traditional church pastor or even a church-planting missionary. Still he knew he was gaining valuable training at the seminary that God would use somehow. He completed his course work and then got a job at WMBI radio station on the campus of Moody Bible Institute in Chicago.

"At first all the knobs and meters on the console in the WMBI control room intimidated me," Ralph recalled. "Even though I was trained as an engineer, it was the most elaborate set-up I'd ever seen. I wondered if I'd ever feel comfortable at the controls."

Ralph soon demonstrated his abilities and ran children's radio dramas such as "Ranger Bill" and "Sailor Sam." He knew his time at the Moody station would be brief, so he made the most of his firsthand experience. As he observed the professionalism of the staff, he made mental notes of how a first-class Christian station is run. In his heart he secretly hoped that one day he could put those principles into practice somewhere— preferably in Alaska. But the Covenant didn't appear to be prepared to establish a radio presence at that time, so Ralph knew he would just have to venture through whatever doors God opened.

That anticipated guidance came by way of a phone call before his year was up at WMBI. WHJC, a Christian radio station in an Appalachian coal-mining town of Matewan, West Virginia, needed an engineer. The Fondells accepted the invitation as an answer to their prayers.

In the midst of engineering and announcing at WHJC, Ralph and Gert felt like real-life missionaries, since many non-Christians listened to the Christian programming. It was there that Gert made her broadcasting debut in addition to mothering three children under four. Substituting occasionally for the host of a program called "Lines from a Mother's Scrapbook," she offered listeners a glimpse into what she was learning firsthand about trusting God with issues of family life.

In addition to work around the station, the Fondells invested themselves on weekends at a nearby coal mining camp. Ralph led a Sunday school at the camp. He was preacher and Bible teacher, while Gert served as Sunday-school superintendent and pianist.

Ralph loved his work. It was a confirmation of his call to serve God through broadcasting. But West Virginia wasn't Alaska. His longings to be a pioneer broadcaster in the Arctic continued to grow. About this time Ralph's aunt, who worked as a nurse in Sitka, Alaska, saw a notice in the local paper announcing a position at a Presbyterian-owned radio station in town. She wrote to her nephew, and immediately Ralph began the process of applying for the position.

While Ralph was still filling out forms, he learned of a job opening at a Christian radio station in Kentucky that would offer him more responsibility and allow him to expand his knowledge of engineering. Ralph was unsure what to do. He had a chance to go to Alaska, but he also had a chance to gain valuable experience. Ralph and Gert prayed about what to do. When the Kentucky station manager indicated the job might only be only a few months in duration, Ralph felt he had his answer—he could accomplish the job in Kentucky in a short period of time, and still be available to move to Alaska. He continued the process of application for the Sitka station.

After four years in West Virginia, the Fondells packed up their belongings and headed to Kentucky. "The studio was in an old house," Ralph recalls. "The control room was in the kitchen where flattened-out cardboard boxes, chicken wire, and burlap were used as acoustical treatment. I knew we were still in rural America when I heard cows mooing outside during my newscasts or watched mice scurrying across the chicken wire on the studio ceiling."

The assignment that was to last only three months lasted almost two years. Although Ralph was unable to follow through on the job opportunity in Sitka, he continued to be grateful for the valuable experience he was obtaining as a chief engineer. In that capacity he was called on to install a new transmitter, increase the station's power from 250 to 1,000 watts, and repair the tower.

Meanwhile, more than 3,000 miles away in Alaska a series of parallel developments were taken place that indicated God was indeed pouring the foundation for a radio station in Nome.

CHAPTER FOUR

Waiting as Momentum Builds

A week or two of gliding through the Alaskan wilderness at subzero temper-
atures with bone-chilling winds can take an emotional toll. To make sure that
mushers maintain their mental and physical health, Iditarod officials require
that sled drivers factor in rest along the 1,100-mile trail. Twice they must stop
to cool their heels (and those of their dogs) by stopping for a minimum of eight
hours. Mushers are permitted to decide where and when one of those pit stops
will occur. The second eight-hour time-out must take place at White Mountain,
a village on the Fish River, near the head of Golovin Lagoon, seventy miles
from Nome.

In addition to the two mandatory eight-hour layovers, the rules of the race
also require mushers to rest their dogs for twenty-fours at a checkpoint of their
choice. The conditions of the trail or the weather often dictate when rest will
come.

E verett Bachelder was a missionary affiliated with the Plymouth
Brethren and a veteran dog musher. Ever since graduating from
the Bible Institute of Los Angeles in 1938, Everett was committed to take
God's word to those who had not heard it. With his lead dog Pinky and
his faithful team, he conducted children's meetings and spoke in church

services in Alaska. He gave demonstrations about dog sleds and distributed tracts that explained the plan of salvation.

Everett also had a passion to reach the Russian people with God's love. One winter he attempted to mush his dog team across the frozen Bering Sea to Siberia. But with land in sight, weather conditions forced him to abandon his daring plan. Resorting to another approach, Everett rolled and inserted Russian gospel tracts into empty glass bottles. He then prayed over them, corked them, and tossed them into the Bering Sea. Amazingly, many bottles actually reached Siberia, and recipients wrote to Everett telling him they had read the tracts.

In 1954 Everett, now married and with a growing family, moved to Nome. With his wife, Mina, at his side, Everett had a partner with which to explore creative ways of reaching people with the gospel. Two Brethren men stationed at the Air Force base in Nome attended Sunday meetings with the Bachelders. Because they also worked at the Armed Forces radio station, they began to dream with Everett and Mina about the impact that radio might have for Jesus' sake in Alaska. Contact was made with other Plymouth Brethren assemblies in the United States to see if finances might be raised to start a radio ministry.

Meanwhile, Roald Amundsen, pastor of Nome Covenant Church, continued to contemplate how Covenant mission stations could benefit from radio. His experience with the local Air Force station only served to strengthen his conviction that radio was an essential tool in such a remote location. Although the 1945 radio committee had determined that a radio station was not at the time feasible, Roald, like Ralph Hanson before him, was convinced that Christian broadcasting was needed to tie all the missions together and to encourage pastors and believers. Whenever he got the chance he talked to denominational officials, but, in light of the recommendations of the 1945 committee, the denomination was reluctant to move forward.

The Nome Ministerial Association continued to take advantage of free airtime on the local military station and provided weekly devotional programming. By this time the Air Force base had moved out to the airport, making the weekly trek to the studio more difficult for the ministers to make, especially in the harsh Nome winters. The Covenant parsonage was more centrally located for these broadcasts, so Roald approached the authorities at the base to see if a small studio could be set up in his home. The base officials agreed.

In addition to being a pastor, Roald was a bush pilot, and he understood the importance of radio telephone equipment. Radio telephones operate much like walkie-talkies. They transmit and receive messages, and only one user can speak at a time. Without them, pilots could leave on a two-week trip and no one would know if they had arrived at their destination or crashed. Two weeks could pass without confirmation of arrival. Roald realized that what aided pilots as they navigated in treacherous weather and terrain could also benefit those at the various mission stations isolated from one another. At this time villages of western Alaska did not have standard land-line phone services and communication between Covenant mission stations was limited to mail and visits. If the Covenant could get its own radio phone system in place, it would help connect the local churches and their pastors. But that kind of equipment was expensive.

Roald and Harriet Amundsen and family

In the summer of 1955 Roald spoke at the Covenant church in Lafayette, California, near San Francisco. A man named Bill Hartman heard him speak of the need in Alaska for radio telephones. He felt he could help in some way. Like Ralph Fondell, Bill had trained as a radio technician in the Navy. He had also gained valuable experience in radio transmission while working for the Forest Service in Texas. But he didn't have a sizable bank account and he didn't have access to the equipment needed. "The Lord could provide a solution," he thought. "If God wants me to help, he can provide the means." As he shared his dream, Bill enlisted others from his church with a background in radio electronics.

Together, Bill and his friends formed what they called the Alaska Radio Committee. With Bill as chairperson, the committee contacted Ralph Hanson in Chicago. Seeing an opportunity to further his vision for a radio station in Nome, Ralph encouraged them to continue working directly with Roald Amundsen. He understood how important radio phone communication would be to the mission. Also, if the radio phone system proved economically and technically feasible, then maybe he could convince the Covenant missions board to pursue his vision of a Christian broadcast station.

In September 1955 the committee met with Roald to outline the operational needs of the Alaska mission. They mapped out a communications plan that would meet the unique demands of the Covenant villages. Then they made an exciting discovery.

"It was truly amazing," Bill recalled later. "After much prayer and investigating leads we found a dozen six-channel transmitters. The U.S. Signal Corps had classified them as surplus even though they had never been used."

The transmitters were ideally suited to the needs of the north and were worth several hundred dollars each. Thanks to funds from the denomination, a gift from the Pasadena Covenant Church in California, and the generous support of individual Covenanters such as Wally Lindskoog of Turlock, California, the committee had sufficient funds to purchase all twelve transmitter sets for $100 each.

The group was ecstatic. They knew how a system of radio telephones would allow the isolated mission stations to communicate with each other.

Bill
Hartman

Still they were aware that these transmitters were only the beginning of what was needed to make the system operational. Additional equipment and work would be required. Thus began several months of working together in evenings and on weekends in one another's basements and workshops. Together, Bill and his friends built power supplies, reground crystals, built and installed modulation limiters consistent with Federal Communications Commission (FCC) standards, and found receivers compatible with the transmitters. By June 1956 they had sent ten crates of equipment to Alaska. Although it was a far cry from a broadcast ministry using a radio station, Covenant missionaries would be able to communicate with one another more efficiently.

Roald called Bill to tell him the crates had arrived and to express his gratitude. He also acknowledged one additional need. Now that he had the equipment in hand, he needed help installing it. In all of western Alaska there was not a licensed technician to be found. Even though Roald had the technical know-how as a Ham radio operator, he was not legally authorized to sign off on the installations. With a second-class FCC license, Bill was qualified.

As Bill pondered the need, he talked to his wife, Arlene, and daughter, Gail. What if he were to use his three weeks of vacation to go work in Alaska? After much conversation and prayer, the decision was made. Bill would go.

A couple months after the crates left San Francisco Bay, Bill made his way to Nome to supervise the installation of the equipment. As the plane touched down and taxied to a stop in Nome, Bill looked out of the window at the fields of treeless tundra. It was a stark contrast from the beauty of Mt. Diablo and the California Coastal Range. Still Bill saw in the haunting landscape a unique beauty, which was framed by his unshaken confidence that God was in the process of doing a life-changing work in Alaska through a cutting edge technology. Bill stepped off the plane thanking God for the privilege of being part of the process.

Bill installed the first radio telephone in the Amundsens' home next door to the Covenant church. The parsonage would serve as the home base for the new network. Within weeks the mission stations in White Mountain, Unalakleet, and Fortuna Ledge were connected with the new equipment. In addition, mission boats on the Yukon River and one traveling to Nunivak Island were also equipped with radio phones.

"Almost immediately the radio telephones were proving the need for a more expansive radio presence," Bill remembered. "When the autumn temperatures resulted in the Bering Sea and rivers freezing up, mission boats could no longer reach the villages on missions of mercy. Wintry weather also kept planes from flying. But medical emergencies were still occurring. That's where the radio telephones allowed for doctors to walk laypeople through lifesaving procedures."

Radio phone
operator from
Shishmaref

During that winter, when tuberculosis outbreaks required people to be quarantined, the radio transmissions allowed for daily discussion between family members and respective villages. In addition, other medical situations were aided by the new electronic access.

The missionaries were overwhelmed by the work that Bill and his committee had invested in procuring and installing the new equipment. But radio phone communication was not the same as a Christian broadcast station. Roald sensed that Bill was an ally who could help make that dream a reality. For the three weeks Bill was in Alaska, Roald had a captive audience. As they flew from village to village, the entrepreneurial missionary made a convincing case for how the Covenant could benefit from a full-fledged radio ministry. Bill saw first-hand how Christian programming could provide encouragement to the pastors and quality teaching to Christians in the villages where there was no pastor.

"As I think back on Roald's passion for a radio ministry, the pragmatism in the man came through," Bill recalled. "He said a radio station would add a dimension of prestige to the Covenant's work. Smaller groups would be reluctant to go in and start a competing missionary work if the villages were tied together by a broadcasting presence."

Roald was so persuasive that he convinced Bill to stop off in Sitka, Alaska, on his way back to California to observe the operation of the KSEW, a radio station operated by the Presbyterian Church. It was the station Ralph Fondell had considered working for. Roald also urged Bill to use his expertise to write a feasibility report for a radio ministry in Alaska. With his impressions of western Alaska, Bill returned to California convinced that the presence of the new electronic communication system was only a stop-gap measure. He concurred with Roald's assessment that the mission needed more than the means to transmit personal messages. He agreed that a radio station was necessary to link the villages together through inspirational music, Christian teaching, local and national news, as well as the kind of communication that radio telephones allowed for.

Bill spent considerable time during the winter of 1956-57 writing a proposal for a Covenant radio station in Nome. The proposal included power recommendation, suggested frequency, and other technical issues. Most importantly, Bill made his own case for the Covenant to take a fresh look at the need for a radio station in western Alaska. Still feeling the rush of emotion from his recent trip, he contended that there was no better opportunity than now. Bill sent the proposal to Ralph Hanson in Chicago.

For more than a decade, Ralph, ever the advocate for Alaska missions, had never given up hope on the Alaska radio project. Funding and staffing issues inevitably kept revived interest from moving ahead. But as the denominational head of missions read Bill Hartman's proposal, something stirred within him. He couldn't help but wonder if this was an idea whose time had finally come.

"Always before the proposal had seemed far too much for us to undertake," Ralph recalled. "Yet at the same time there has always been a sense of destiny. I couldn't help but think that God was in it."

Roald, who had received a copy of Bill's proposal, also felt that the time was right. In early 1957, he wrote a letter to Ralph Hanson telling him the need for a Christian broadcast station was greater now than ever. Most importantly, the Covenant needed a tool to support Alaska Native pastors in their own languages. Roald also argued that a radio station could be an effective evangelism tool. Finally, he reminded Ralph of Axel Karlson's vision by saying that a radio ministry would "once again open to us the Far East and many places in Siberia."

The combination of Bill's proposal and Roald's letter convinced Ralph to act. In his April 17, 1957 report on Alaska to the Covenant Board of Foreign Missions, he made his plea. Quoting extensively from Roald's passionate letter, Ralph acknowledged the concerns raised by the 1945 radio committee, but he stated that he believed there were qualified people to staff a station and also individuals within the Covenant who would support it financially. Most importantly, he told the board that he sensed divine guidance for starting the project now. He concluded his report by saying:

> For years Covenant Men [a denominational organization] have felt the need for a really challenging project which would stir the imagination and rally support, giving this organization a sense of mission and achievement. An Alaska radio project would be extremely challenging yet within the means of this organization.... operating a mission radio station capable of reaching northwestern Alaska and also reaching deeply into Soviet Siberia would be tremendously challenging to our entire Covenant.

Ralph's report proved persuasive. The board approved the recommendation and passed it on to the Covenant Executive Board, which brought it to the delegates at the 1957 Covenant Annual Meeting for a vote. The recommendation indicated that the Alaska Missionary Council was not only behind this project but was willing to have all of the $15,000 that was allocated for Alaska from the Covenant's seventy-fifth anniversary Diamond Jubilee fund go toward the start-up costs for the radio ministry. The recommendation concluded by saying:

> This year, 1957, marks the seventieth anniversary of our Alaska mission field, and it seems fitting that we should launch out upon some challenging new project as a memorial of gratitude to God. There appears to be a number of significant evidences that God is placing such a challenging opportunity before us in this proposed missionary radio sta-

tion. We, therefore, recommend that authorization be granted the Board of Missions and the Executive Board to continue studying the possibility of establishing a missionary radio station at or near Nome, Alaska; to take the necessary preliminary steps, including the filing of application with the Federal Communications Commission for licensing if deemed advisable; and to report detailed findings to the 1958 Annual Meeting.

The recommendation was unanimously passed.

At the same time that interest for a radio ministry in Alaska was being renewed in Chicago, Ralph and Gert Fondell received, in January 1957, a belated Christmas card from Don Bruckner. Once Ralph's classmate at North Park College, Don was now a missionary in Alaska. Since he was aware of Ralph's ongoing interest in a broadcast ministry in the northland, he wrote to notify his old college chum of the exciting developments. Don suggested Ralph contact Roald Amundsen.

Ralph and Gert Fondell

Ralph wasted no time in responding. For him, Don's letter was an answer to prayer. Just two months earlier, the Fondells had been given assurance that the Lord was still at work on their behalf to open the door to Alaska. One morning while having her devotions, Gert sensed that God was using this lengthy season of waiting to increase their patience and trust in him. Gert read, "You need to persevere so that when you have done the will of God, you will receive what he has promised" (Hebrews 10:36).

In his letter to Roald, Ralph wrote, "I am very interested in missionary radio and especially so in Alaska. In fact, I have in the past considered making application for a position as engineer at KSEW in Sitka, Alaska, under the Presbyterian Board of National Missions. However, as I am a member of the Covenant, I am much more interested in Covenant missions. But my desire is to serve Christ where he leads."

Roald responded on the same day he received the letter. He also wrote to Bill Hartman, telling him about the Fondells. Bill proceeded to contact Ralph and Gert. Roald also alerted Ralph Hanson in Chicago to Ralph Fondell's interest. But it was Fondell's telegram to Hanson in the fall that prompted the elder Ralph to respond.

Hanson updated Fondell on where the radio project stood. Even though the 1957 Covenant Annual Meeting had passed the recommendation on pursuing an Alaska radio project, Hanson was noticeably cautious in his communication with the Fondells. While the missions office and the Covenant Executive Board had been authorized to continue to study the project as well as to apply to the FCC for a license, Hanson was not yet in a position to invite the Fondells to leave Kentucky.

Hanson's response was all Ralph and Gert needed to begin to mentally pack their bags. Despite the cautionary tone of the letter, they felt their dream would soon be realized.

A veteran missionary broadcaster by the name of Art Zylstra also had his sights on the Arctic. In World War II he received radio and radar training and served as the radio operator on a small ship in the Pacific. During his term of duty, Art prayed to God that if he returned home safely, he would dedicate his life to using Christian radio as a tool to win souls to Christ. Upon his return from the war, Art, a native of Lynden, Washington, transferred from Seattle Pacific College to John Brown University in

Art Zylstra (far right) in Quito, Ecuador

Siloam Springs, Arkansas, were he could major in radio broadcasting and work at the radio station on campus.

Like Ralph Fondell, Art worked at WMBI in Chicago after college. But remembering his promise to God, he responded to a need he had heard about at HCJB radio in Quito, Ecuador, "The Voice of the Andes." During the war Art had been stationed at Treasure Island in San Francisco Bay, California, and had been attending Mission Covenant Church in Oakland, where he had met his wife, Margaret. The Covenant denomination commissioned Art and Margaret as missionaries and then loaned them to World Radio Missionary Fellowship, the world's largest mission radio organization, which operated HCJB. While in Quito they helped to start a small Covenant church.

In 1954 Art accepted an offer to become station manager of HOXO "The Voice of the Isthmus" in Panama. His gregarious personality and leadership abilities soon found Art presiding over the Pan-American Christian Network of radio stations.

Ralph Hanson recognized that Art was the logical choice to lead the Covenant radio station in Alaska. In 1957, when the Zylstras were on furlough, Ralph contacted Art to see if he would consider giving leadership to the emerging Alaska radio project. Art and Margaret committed to pray separately for two days and then come back together on the third day to discuss the opportunity. On the third day they were both convinced that God was leading them to Alaska. Art let Ralph know of their decision. Hanson and the Covenant Board of Missions then asked World Radio Missionary Fellowship to release the Zylstras for two to four years to work on the Alaska radio project. World Radio Missionary Fellowship granted this request.

So in the fall of 1957 Bill Hartman and Art Zylstra went to work. Together they focused on preparing the application to the FCC for a license. One of the first issues to consider was whether the denomination would hold the license or should it create a separate nonprofit organization for that purpose. In October 1957 Art met with Joseph P. Zias of the Washington, D.C. law firm of Loucks, Zias, Young, and Jansky. Zias had come highly recommended not only as an expert in the laws surrounding commercial radio, but specifically as an expert in processing applications submitted by groups that operated Christian commercial stations.

Zias suggested that the Covenant Church form a subsidiary corporation whose sole objective would be owning and operating of the radio station. Thus, Arctic Broadcasting Association (ABA) was born. ABA was formed as a not-for-profit, tax-exempt corporation, which allowed it to accept tax deductible donations to support its work. As a subsidiary corporation of the Covenant, ABA was connected to the Covenant and their missionary work in Alaska in such a manner that ensured that the station would remain responsive to the needs of the Covenant Church in western Alaska.

With these matters decided, Art turned his attention to finding a chief engineer for the project. In November 1957, Art contacted Ralph Fondell by letter. "If this radio project goes through," he wrote, "I'd hope you would agree to be my chief engineer." Although he had been dreaming of such an opportunity for the better part of ten years, Ralph wondered if he had the ability to build a tower on the tundra, and guarantee that the project that has taken so long to get off the ground would succeed. His self-effacing doubts soon dissipated. The Holy Spirit began to quicken within him a sense of confidence and inner peace. He realized that he did not have to guarantee the project's success. God would do that. All he had to do was be faithful and available to the ministry.

By the spring of 1958, the denomination was moving ahead with plans to build a station in Nome. Bill's and Art's hard work proved that the station was technically feasible and the FCC application process was well under way. With Art on board as general manager and Ralph Fondell as chief engineer, the staffing was in place. As for financing, the denomination had already received over $20,000 in donations toward the project. Art and Ralph Hanson would propose to the delegates at the upcoming 1958 Annual Meeting that the total project costs of $60,000 be spread over two budget years with roughly two thirds being spent in 1958 and the remaining one third in 1959. It was clear to them that God's hand was moving this project forward in ways that had not been evident back in 1945 when the radio committee recommended against pursing a radio ministry in Alaska. They were confident that the Annual Meeting would approve the proposed budget for the project.

But there was one problem that had to do with the timing of the Annual Meeting and the brief summer season in Nome. Staff housing had to be built in the summer of 1958 so that when the Fondell family arrived in the spring of 1959, Ralph could focus on building the broadcast tower and necessary buildings at the transmitter site. Because there are only a couple of months in the year when the Bering Sea is thawed and barges with supplies are able sail into Nome from Seattle, the construction materials for the housing would have to be purchased and shipped in the spring, before the Annual Meeting had approved a budget for the station.

While speaking in the Seattle area, Art shared the situation with George Lagerquist, a Christian and local businessman. Lagerquist showed uncharacteristic interest in Art's story. "Do you know what kind of work I'm in?" he asked Art. As Art shook his head, Lagerquist explained. "I'm in construction materials and most of my customers are in Alaska." George Lagerquist owned Galco Wood Products.

Art didn't exactly know what Lagerquist was getting at, but as they talked he had a sense that God was present in this meeting, providing a solution to what Art had thought was an impossible situation.

"Do you think the Covenant denomination will approve the radio project and fund the cost of materials and transportation?" Lagerquist asked him.

"I believe it with all my heart," Art confidently replied.

"Then I don't see a problem," his new friend explained. "If you give me a list of the materials you need for the first phase of your project, I will make sure everything gets loaded on the first barge headed for Nome. That way your supplies will arrive in time for the construction season."

Willing to be reimbursed following the Annual Meeting's decision, George Lagerquist agreed to purchase the supplies himself. It was a remarkable answer to prayer. It was one of many as the momentum to create a radio ministry in Nome began to build.

Facing Impossible Odds

The name Alaska comes from an Aleut word that means "the great land." Not only is it great in terms of its size and unique beauty, it also conjures up images of great challenge. Every year, adventurers attempt to reach the 20,320-foot peak of Mt. McKinley or snowshoe over the Mendenhall Glacier, one of 100,000 glaciers in the state. But they do so at great risk.

It was another great challenge that Libby Riddles faced in the 1985 Iditarod. While other mushers waited out a blinding blizzard, Riddles left Shaktoolik when the storm was just beginning. She knew she was taking an enormous risk, but having gained the lead, she was determined to keep it. Riddles had something to prove. A woman had never won the Iditarod. Although she was taking a great chance, her risk paid off. As a result of mushing through the night barely able to see the trail markers, Libby Riddles crossed the burled arch on Front Street first.

On Thursday June 19, 1958, at the second business session of the 73rd Covenant Annual Meeting, Ralph Hanson, with Art Zylstra at his side, presented the recommendation from the Board of Missions, with concurrence from the Covenant Executive Board, that delegates give final authorization to begin the Alaska radio project. In his report to the delegates he stated: "We have pursued this matter during the past year and, in view of the great need for such a facility, resources in the way of both finances and personnel placed at our command, and many indications of divine guidance, we have proceeded to fulfill the detailed requisites for filing application with the FCC for permission to construct and operate such a station." After Art answered a number of questions from the delegates the motion was put to a vote and was adopted.

The Annual Meeting also commissioned the Fondells as career missionaries with the Covenant, and the Fondells and the Zylstras, who were already commissioned, were consecrated for service in Alaska. That meant the Fondells could take their first step toward Alaska by packing up their belongings and moving their four children from Kentucky to live with Ralph's family in Minnesota.

With the construction materials needed to build the staff housing delivered to Alaska, Ralph and Art approached the next pressing issue on their lengthy to do list—locating property for the transmitter and tower. They needed to find out if there was any land surrounding Nome that was relatively free of permafrost, sub-surface ground that remains frozen year round. Because the top level of soil and rock thaws during the summer only to re-freeze in the winter, the ground twists and buckles, wreaking havoc on roads, parking lots, or building foundations, causing structures to collapse. The projected radio tower and transmitter buildings needed to be constructed on permafrost-free ground if at all possible.

Contacts in Nome advised Art and Ralph to hire a drilling rig and crew, survey the area, and find the most stable location. They indicated that such a procedure could last as long as two years. The men were alarmed. They felt they couldn't wait that long, now that the denomination had finally given them the go ahead.

Art sent letters to a number of military and government offices, hoping to find available information about the terrain in Nome. A response from the Geological Survey in Washington, D.C. was particularly helpful. The letter provided the name and address of a surveyor who had spent two summers drilling in and around Nome. Amazingly enough, the man lived less than twenty minutes away from the Zylstras' California home.

Art contacted the surveyor, who invited him to his home. Art discovered that the man was a Christian. Not only was he genuinely excited about the Covenant's plan to build a radio station in Nome, he was all smiles as he rolled out a geological map of the Norton Sound region and provided Art the information he needed.

"Mr. Zylstra," he began. "In the area in which you and your denomination want to locate a transmitter and tower, my studies have revealed there is only one place relatively free from permafrost. It is right here."

Using a pencil, the surveyor pointed to a small parcel of land southeast of the Nome city limits where the Nome River flowed out into the Bering Sea. The information that could have taken months (if not years) to discover, had been found.

With ever-growing confidence that God was blessing their efforts, Ralph and Art said goodbye to their families and met in Seattle before flying north for the summer. The two had not yet been to Alaska, and in fact had only just met face to face at the 1958 Annual Meeting. All contact work had been done from a distance. As the plane began its approach to the Anchorage airport, the men looked out of the window. The sight was breathtaking. The snow-capped mountains of the Chugach mountain range appeared to be scraping the bottom of the fuselage. The grandeur of the mountains reflected the incredible greatness of the Creator, on whose power they had come to rely for each step of the radio venture.

In Anchorage, Ralph and Art changed to a smaller plane for the flight to Nome. As they flew over the massive Alaska Range, they noticed how dramatically the landscape below them changed. The terrain through which the Yukon River flowed was flat and treeless.

Before arriving in Nome, the plane had a stop in Unalakleet. Upon landing there, one of the plane's tires blew out. The pilot was able to safely bring the plane to a stop on the small runway, but the scheduled continuation to Nome was delayed a day while a new tire was flown in from Anchorage. Art and Ralph made the best of the unexpected layover. They shared a meal with pioneer Covenant missionary L. E. Ost (who had first arrived in western Alaska in 1910) and Maynard Londborg, who gave leadership to the Covenant high school there. They also walked around the village, engaging people in conversation. Ralph visited Steffan Katchatag.

"I will never forget meeting Mr. Katchatag," Ralph recalled. "Art and I were told about this dear brother in Christ who was housebound due to severe physical disabilities. As we visited with him in his home, we described what we had come to Alaska to do. His face lit up with excitement. He had picked up sporadic Christian broadcasts on his shortwave radio."

Most villages in western Alaska were only able to pick up shortwave broadcast stations, which broadcast in higher frequencies than AM stations. These higher frequencies make it possible for people to hear the station many hundreds or even thousands of miles away. As a result, these stations were most often located far from Alaska and their programming was not tailored to the needs of these remote Alaskan villages.

Steffan Katchatag understood that with a station based in Nome, his need for consistent and relevant Christian programming would be met. His words to Ralph were encouraging: "Although your station isn't yet on the air, I know the programs you will broadcast will nourish my soul. They will be daily bread from heaven."

The next day, on July 22, Art and Ralph reached their destination. The town wasn't quite what they had expected. The former boom town of 20,000 residents with its fancy restaurants and hotels was a sleepy little town of about 3,000, without paved streets. Parallel to the driftwood-strewn beach along the Bering Sea was the infamous Front Street of gold rush days. Though a fraction of the size it once was, it still boasted false-front buildings that resembled the main street of a wild-west town. The Board of Trade Saloon continued to bear witness to a permissive and promiscuous past. On the side of the wooden building was painted "Sin City." It and half a dozen other taverns up and down the street seemed

Steffan Katchatag
from Unalakleet

to do a healthy business.

That part hadn't changed from when Wyatt Earp lived in Nome (having given up gun-slinging to open a hotel and casino). What was different was that sixty years earlier the people who were staggering in and out of the bars day and night were gold hungry miners. Now it was Alaska Natives without jobs and seemingly without much purpose in life.

The *Nome Nugget* newspaper office stood out. A sign in the window called attention to the fact it was the oldest continuously published paper in Alaska. It was also the only consistent source of local, state, and national news in town.

Ralph Fondell (left) and Art Zylstra in front of Nome Covenant Church

The two newcomers introduced themselves around town. They had much to do in a small amount of time. They went to the U.S. commissioner's office to find out whether the property that had been identified by the surveyor as relatively permafrost-free was claimed by someone else. The commissioner assured them that the land they needed had not been claimed.

Although this odd, pie-shaped piece was larger than they needed, Art and Ralph were ecstatic. They immediately went out to the site and pounded a stake into the ground where the transmitter and tower would be located. It was an acceptable way of staking it out until application for ownership could be formally made. Like the memorial stones set by the Old Testament patriarchs as a witness to God's deliverance, the marker called attention to God's faithfulness.

The balance of that summer was spent helping Spencer Strand, a Covenant missionary, build two homes for the Fondell and Zylstra families. For one of the homes, Spencer actually used a miner's shack built during the gold rush as the main structure.

In late October 1958, after they said goodbye to their new friends in Nome, Art and Ralph stopped in Fairbanks to visit the Bureau of Land Management Office to apply for the land they had staked in Nome. After submitting the necessary documentation, they asked how long it would take for the application papers to be processed. The answer was like a blow to the stomach. It would take up to two years. Leaving the building, they proceeded to kneel on the ground and pray that God would intervene.

Art Zylstra stakes claim to the land for the KICY transmitter site.

Ralph and Art left Alaska to rejoin their respective families. The plan called for the Fondell family to move to Nome in the summer of 1959 and the Zylstra family to join them in the fall. That would allow them to get established and complete the construction of the studio before the station would go on the air sometime in the spring of 1960.

Until that time, Ralph and Art traveled extensively, speaking in Covenant churches throughout the denomination to raise awareness as well as funds for the Alaska radio project. Following a presentation in Minnesota, Art connected with the son of a former associate at WMBI. When he asked where the man's parents were now living and what they were doing, he was dumbfounded to discover they were living in Fairbanks, where Art's old friend was working for the Bureau of Land Management. Art told the son that he had visited that very office only a few months earlier while trying to secure ownership of a very valuable piece of property.

The young man wrote to his parents about his unexpected encounter with Art Zylstra. He told his father of Art's concern about the time it would take to process the paperwork for the land deed. Within a couple weeks, Art received a letter from this friend he hadn't seen in years. "I've put a special tag on your file so that it will stay at the top of the heap," his friend wrote. "As God would have it, I am temporarily serving in a capacity within the bureau where I can help you. Ordinarily I would not have that ability."

He ended the letter by writing, "Although there are lots of places I would rather be just now, I don't believe it's happenstance that I am here. If the Lord can use me to help this thing along, I'll feel it's been worthwhile."

When Art read those words, the 6'5" missionary broadcaster felt more like ten feet tall.

On Palm Sunday evening, Art, Ralph and Gert Fondell, and Howie and Pat Nelson (who were to be commissioned as missionaries at the 1959 Annual Meeting to work on the Alaska radio project) were scheduled to be at First Covenant Church in Des Moines, Iowa, for a special evening service. But a couple of days before that meeting, Ralph got an unexpected call. Art had suffered a severe heart attack and was hospitalized in Chicago. Ralph was asked to fly to Kansas City to preach at First Covenant Church in place of Art on Palm Sunday morning and then fly on to Des Moines for the Sunday evening service. As Ralph stood before the two congregations, he asked for prayer for his colleague in ministry. With Art's health at risk, many contingency plans were considered. Fortunately, Art recovered quickly and the plans for both families to move continued.

Ralph and Gert Fondell and family

In the summer of 1959, Ralph and Gert and their four children, accompanied by Art, arrived in the largest, northernmost, and westernmost state of the union. Only months earlier, on January 3, 1959, Alaska had become the forty-ninth state. They arrived in Fairbanks, where the land manager had good news for them. Not only had the application for the property they staked out been approved, but since the property was going to be used for religious purposes, the land was available at half its commercial value.

In Nome, the situation was not as encouraging, however. Soon after the Fondells arrived, Ralph discovered that the town was unable to provide the transmitter site with power. He realized that their only option was to buy a diesel generator. Ralph called Art, who had returned to California for a medical check-up and to attend the birth of his daughter. The call came none too soon. The last Nome-bound barge of the season was being loaded in Elliott Bay in Seattle. There was no time to lose. Art located the necessary equipment and made arrangements for it to be shipped to Seattle and delivered to the appropriate pier. Then he phoned the Alaska Steamship Company to alert them to the delivery that needed to be added to the final shipment. Still savoring a sense of satisfaction at having successfully located the portable power plant, Art wasn't prepared for the clerk's blunt reply. No more cargo was being loaded for Nome. Once again, Art prayed fervently for God to intervene. Without the generator the radio project would be delayed for several months.

A few days later Art drove to Pier 43 in Seattle and saw that the crated diesel generator had been delivered. It was sitting outside a closed gate. As he raced into the shipping office, he heard someone call out his name. "Art Zylstra, what are you doing here?" Art turned to find an old Navy chum he hadn't seen in fifteen years. The man was an employee of the shipping company. When Art explained his predicament, his friend excused himself, and left the room to make a phone call. When he came back, he directed Art to the window where the two watched the locked gate open and a forklift load the crate onto the barge.

One breakthrough after another marked the preliminary steps in the radio station's development, giving Ralph and Art the encouragement they needed after an exhausting year of planning and itineration. But for Ralph Hanson, the denominational missions executive who had dreamed

Survey of KICY transmitter site

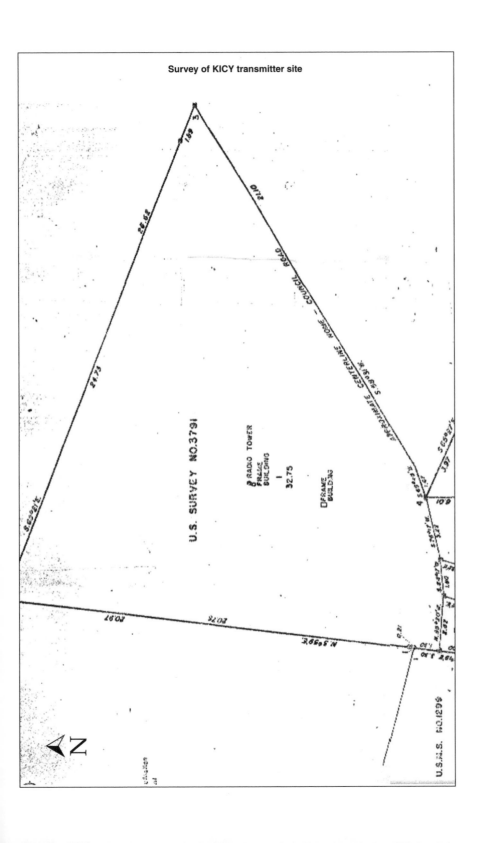

of a radio station in Alaska for almost twenty-five years, the Divine fingerprints were a much needed validation of his vision.

With the power source for the future radio transmitter en route to Nome, Ralph and Gert and their family began to settle in. Their home was the turn-of-the-century gold rush shack Ralph, Art, and Spencer Strand had reinforced the previous summer. One major adjustment the family had to make was to the never-ending Arctic daylight. On a typical summer night the sun did not go down until after midnight. And even at that, the sky didn't get fully dark before the sun reappeared a couple hours later. With no school to get up for, the Fondell children rode their bikes and played in the street long past dinner just like the other kids in the neighborhood. Gert experimented with light-blocking techniques. Newspaper and cardboard in the windows helped create some semblance of darkness.

While Gert helped the children find a new rhythm to their transplanted lives, Ralph focused on the task of assembling the transmission tower, which had been shipped from Seattle weeks earlier. Fortunately for Ralph, Bill Hartman agreed to return that summer for two weeks and help construct the tower. He timed his arrival to coincide with the arrival of the barge carrying the unassembled tower. What he found was not quite what he had expected.

"I naively thought that the radio tower would be unloaded in sections ready to be put up," Bill later recalled. "But that wasn't the way it was at all. Instead I saw a pile of small boxes and crates containing pieces of the tower on the beach. It was scattered on the beach along with everything else the barge had unloaded. There among the boxed clothing, food, and household supplies people in Nome had ordered for the coming winter was a gigantic erector set waiting to be unpacked and assembled."

Missing from the array of containers was an instruction manual. The boxes of tower parts were trucked to the Covenant surplus hangar on an airstrip east of town. There, Ralph and Bill went to work. Slowly, by trial and error, they came up with a system for bolting the unpainted parts together in a way that resembled what they knew the finished product should look like. In order to keep the sections from becoming too heavy to maneuver, they limited them to ten-foot lengths.

But before attempting to assemble the tower sections vertically, they had to paint the steel so that the 250-foot tower could be clearly seen by pilots taking off and landing and to prevent rusting. They had not anticipated that the parts would come unpainted. Ralph and Bill found plenty of white paint in town, but they also needed "international orange" paint, a color required by both the Federal Communications Commission and the Federal Aviation Administration. There was no orange paint for sale in town. It could not be flown in because paint was considered a hazardous material, and it could not be shipped in because the last barge of the season had already left Seattle. Fortunately, the local road department was willing to loan cans of bright orange paint to the desperate workers until a barge the following spring could deliver more.

Re-enter Everett Bachelder. When the musher-missionary in town realized that the Covenant was moving full-speed ahead on bringing a radio station into reality, he offered to help in any way he could. His dreams for a Plymouth Brethren radio ministry had faded when the Covenant submitted its application for an FCC license. Still, when he learned that tower sections needed to be painted, he stepped forward to do the job.

While Everett sloshed white and orange paint in alternating bands on the ten-foot sections, Ralph and Bill studied aerial photographs that indicated where the tower and the supporting guy wires should be positioned. Although the tower's center pier would be located on a section of permafrost-free tundra, the steel wires extending out would not necessarily be. The two men examined the photos for evidence of blueberry patches. Because blueberries have a root structure, their presence would indicate soil more easily penetrable than permanently frozen tundra where only grasses could grow on the surface.

Tower building crew in the summer of 1959

With schematic drawings of where the guy wires should be anchored in hand, Ralph and Bill supervised a handful of volunteers who had paid their own way to Nome for a few weeks. The team dug a series of holes that were five feet deep and poured concrete. There could be no scrimping here. The guy wires would be critical to keeping the tower erect and immovable in the notorious Arctic winds that blow during the winter.

When the holes were dug, Ralph and Bill began hoisting the ten-foot sections of tower with 5/16 inch rope they had located in town. They would climb the tower together, bolting the sections into place as the ground crew hoisted them up using a home-made pulley system. Reaching dizzying heights, the two climbed the growing white and orange monolith day after day.

Bill Hartman and Ralph Fondell assembled the 250-foot tower in 10-foot sections.

The construction of the studio building was taking shape half a block from the gray house where the Fondells lived. With Spencer Strand supervising the operation, volunteers from Covenant churches in Washington and California worked to frame the exterior building and then the interior control room from which the programming would eventually originate.

When the time came for Bill and the other volunteers to return home, there was a change in the weather. Rain, wind, and even snow showers signaled a temporary end to the summer projects. As Ralph said a grateful goodbye to a cadre of weary workers returning to the lower forty-eight, he was finally able to breathe a sigh of relief. The 200-foot tower standing proudly above the old gold rush community silently announced that the long awaited radio project was at last coming to pass. With the guy wires anchored into place, there was no reason to think the new radio tower was going anywhere.

Although there was still fifty more feet of tower to cap off the project, Ralph was grateful for a couple days of inclement weather. The thirty-six-year-old engineer was exhausted. When the weather improved on the last day of August, Ralph was ready to get back up on the tower and finish the final five sections by himself. Before heading off to the transmitter site that morning, Gert and Ralph sat at the kitchen table for devotions. They discovered that the ministry highlighted in the *Covenant Prayer Book* for that day was the Alaska radio project. As he spent the next six hours on the tower, Ralph was sustained by the knowledge that hundreds of Covenanters in the United States and Canada were praying for him and his family.

When the instructions for assembling the tower finally arrived weeks after the initial shipment, Ralph realized that they had assembled it backwards! But no matter, with inventive ingenuity, Ralph and Bill had built a tower that would stand for many years.

Once the tower was up, volunteers from the Nome Covenant Church began laying ground wire and the all-important ground system. These wires had to be stretched in uniform distances away from the base of the tower. It was a time-consuming effort. By the middle of September, construction was complete on the transmitter building and the building to house the diesel generator.

As Art and Margaret Zylstra and their four children flew into Nome in mid-October, the 250-foot lighted tower welcomed them to a town surrendering to the chill and the fast approaching darkness of winter. It was a winter that would conclude with an Easter sunrise never to be forgotten.

CHAPTER SIX

Laying a Firm Foundation

Although all Iditarod mushers dream of one day winning first place, that is not the primary motivator for most of them. It is the joy and the challenge of the journey that sustains them during the rigorous months of training leading up to the race. At certain checkpoints along the way, the mushers are required to sign-in and initial documents. There they take time to check the dogs for injury, feed them, and rest them for a brief time.

Because residents and fans crowd around the individual mushers, most racers will acknowledge them as they attempt to make up lost time while signing the paperwork on the fly. Some mushers will give autographs. A few are even willing to disregard the ticking clock and engage villagers in meaningful conversation. Mike Williams of Akiak, Alaska, is one such dog driver.

This middle-aged Yupiaq is quite outspoken about his reason for racing each year. He participates in the Iditarod to call attention to the deadly consequences of alcoholism. Having been personally impacted by alcohol, Williams is committed to helping others find the freedom of sobriety. As a result, those who are motivated by his example seek him out as he stops at each village. A committed Christian, Williams takes time from the race to visit with those who are struggling with a disease that has taken a hefty toll on the Alaska Native community.

When Mike Williams eventually arrives in Nome each year, he's not in a hurry to leave. A week after the first musher crosses the finish line, he is one of the Iditarod participants who gladly gives his testimony at Nome Covenant Church on Mushers' Sunday. For Williams, being sensitive to and available for people who look up to him is an important part of the race.

The Fondells welcomed the Zylstra family with open arms. Even though the two families hardly knew each other, the arrival of the Zylstras felt like a family reunion. While Margaret Zylstra took responsibility for getting the family settled, Art didn't waste any time getting reacquainted in town. His outgoing personality served him well as he continued to get to know community leaders and business owners. The manager of the fledgling radio ministry listened as well as talked. He wanted to know what the people in Nome needed from a broadcast operation, since the new station would be the only full service radio station in town.

But Art's informal survey of potential listeners was not limited to Nome. Thanks to Roald Amundsen, Nome Covenant Church's pilot-pastor, Art and Ralph took advantage of the late fall good weather and flew to villages like White Mountain and Golovin to introduce themselves. Often they entered a home to find a radio prominently displayed in the living room or kitchen. Even though programming had been limited to the Armed Forces station or a shortwave signal from far away, radios were seen as a necessary tool to surviving the harsh Arctic winters.

That first winter Ralph and Roald oversaw the set-up of the diesel generator. At the same time, Lyle Stokes, a volunteer from California, helped with the installation of the transmitter. Meanwhile, Art toyed with

The Zylstra family
arrived in Nome in
the fall of 1959.

a name for the new station that would soon be on the air. He wanted something that would be memorable. The call letters of HCJB in Quito were an acronym for Hoy Cristo Jesus Bendice, Spanish for "Today Christ Jesus Blesses." This ministry that would reach around the globe from the mountains of Ecuador also was nicknamed "The Voice of the Andes." The radio ministry he later went to in Panama was HOXO, "The Voice of the Isthmus." Somehow the call letters needed to reflect the unique region in which the signal would be heard.

In the middle of an Alaskan winter, Art considered K-ICY a most appropriate choice. And taking his cue from his former radio assignments, he thought "The Voice of the Arctic" would be a fitting moniker. Ralph and Gert agreed.

The staff worked night and day to prepare the station for a spring launch. The workload was more than they had anticipated. Art and Ralph were grateful that the Covenant had the foresight to call a third full-time couple. Howie and Pat Nelson had arrived in September of 1959, after being commissioned in June at the 1959 Annual Meeting. Whereas Art would serve as KICY's general manager and Ralph would be the chief engineer, Howie would serve as the station's first program director.

Although the Nelsons had spent a year at North Park Seminary, it was Howie's radio training at Brown Institute of Broadcasting in Minneapolis that had prepared him for the unique challenges of KICY. While Pat worked as a nurse at the local hospital, donating her salary to the operation of the station, Howie began negotiating programs and selecting records that KICY could broadcast once it was up and running.

Howie soon discovered that his job description included a whole lot more than programming. Ralph enlisted his help to string cable three and a half miles from the studio building to the transmitter site. Whenever possible, they attached the cable to existing electrical poles. One day as they were hanging the cable on the poles, the temperature dropped past 20 below. Howie was about twenty feet above ground drilling the holes for the hardware to hang the cable. All of a sudden he slid all the way down to the ground. Later they learned that when the temperature is 20 below or colder the spurs they wore on their industrial boots would not stick into a wooden pole. They decided to wait for more moderate weather.

When the line stringing resumed, Ralph and Howie faced a new challenge. As they left the city limits, they ran out of electrical poles on which to hang the cable. They had to lay the insulated cable on the ground. That set-up would work as long as the occasional moose or caribou didn't gnaw through the rubber insulation. Once the line was fully strung, it was time to test the system.

When the tower was assembled, Howie Nelson and Ralph Fondell strung cable from the studio to the transmitter site.

Ralph recalled, "On the day we tested voice signals, Howie and I stood at the base of the tower and spoke into a mike to Art back at the studio. We weren't sure if he'd be able to hear us. But after a few moments of uncomfortable silence, we heard that deep booming voice coming back through our speakers saying, 'Boy, you guys are really making noise!' I remember thinking, 'This is great—I wonder if Alexander Graham Bell felt this great when he first discovered his telephone invention worked!'"

While the excitement and anticipation built in Nome, there was trouble in Chicago. The expenditures made to purchase the necessary, and sometimes unexpected, equipment to run the station exceeded the amount authorized by the 1958 Annual Meeting by $40,000. This caused considerable concern for those who served on the Covenant Executive Board. Ralph Hanson reassured the Covenant's trustees that support for the station was strong in the churches and that many more individuals were expected to pledge their support in the coming months. In a letter to the Board of Missions, which reported to the Covenant Executive Board, dated December 17, 1959, Hanson reminded the board that "God has guided us, removed obstacles, and provided in a marvelous way.... Apparently a higher authority than any of our boards or even the Covenant

Annual Meeting has given us the privilege of launching this project, and we may be confident he will not let us down."

In the end the Covenant trustees realized that with the equipment already in Nome, the license approved, the major expenditures made, and the station ready to go on air, there was little they could do but trust God to see the station through this financial crisis.

As spring approached, the staff in Nome worked from eight in the morning until ten at night to prepare the station for its first broadcast, the date of which was still not set. On Saturday, March 26 they hosted an open house for the community. More than 400 curious neighbors who had seen the studio building on 4th and D streets go up the previous summer were given an opportunity to see what the inside of a radio station looked like.

The next day, following a celebrative morning of worship at Nome Covenant Church, a special dedication service was held at the newly finished studio. A standing-room only crowd listened as several dignitaries called attention to the milestone this new radio station represented in western Alaska. It was not only providing a new way to evangelize and disciple an area that had once only been accessible by dog sled, it was a communication link with the outside world that the villages and towns on the Seward Peninsula and in the Yukon Delta had dreamed about.

Written greetings were read from the mayor of Nome, the governor of Alaska, the state's only member of Congress, and both U.S. senators from Alaska. A reel-to-reel audiotape recorded by Clarence Nelson, then president of the Covenant denomination, was played. In addition, representatives from the Moravian, Friends, and Lutheran missions flew in from Bethel, Kotzebue, Teller, and Brevig Mission to bring personal greetings. Perhaps the most unexpected greeting came from radio station ELWA in Monrovia, Liberia, congratulating the newest member of the global family of Christian broadcasters.

One of the most moving presentations of the day, however, was from the executive secretary of world mission. Ralph Hanson, the former missionary who had dreamed of such a day, stood before the crowd and gave public gratitude to God for bringing the new radio ministry into being. In his resonant baritone voice, Ralph reviewed the history of the Covenant in Alaska, including the special years he and his family spent in White

Mountain and Golovin twenty-five years earlier.

Paul Fryhling, pastor of First Covenant Church in Minneapolis, which had donated money to build the studio building, gave the keynote message, which was entitled "Man's Vision and God's Miracles." He reflected on the impact radio has had on American culture since it made its debut only forty years earlier. There were already a million radios in use and radio broadcasting was experiencing unprecedented growth. The Covenant's willingness to invest in this cutting-edge technology, Fryhling said, was timely and God-ordained.

Paul Fryhling, pastor of First Covenant Church in Minneapolis, was the keynote speaker at the KICY dedication.

Ralph Hanson's pronouncement that God would not take the Covenant this far without seeing the project through to completion proved true. In addition to the $15,000 gift earmarked for KICY by the Covenant's Diamond Jubilee capital campaign, donations of money and equipment from individuals and churches covered the increased start-up expenses of the station.

Not all of the contributions were financial. In the previous year and a half, countless volunteers had flown into Nome at their own expense to assist with a myriad of projects. And not all gifts were from those connected to the Covenant Church. One sizable check came from a nondenominational group in Saudi Arabia who had heard about the pioneer work.

When the final equipment tests were performed, the FCC gave approval for KICY to begin operation the week of April 11. Art convinced the rest of the staff to wait until April 17, Easter Sunday. On that cold Sunday morning in 1960, Art was in the studio before sunrise. He wanted to make sure he had plenty of time to go through the sign-on protocol. At precisely 6 a.m. Bering Time, he flipped the mike switch in the control room to the right, and read a carefully scripted sign-on greeting he had written days before.

"This is the Voice of the Arctic, radio station KICY, initiating with this announcement. KICY is broadcasting with a transmitted power of 5,000 watts. On this, our first day of broadcasting, and daily throughout the weeks and months of the future, you will be able to tune this frequency for the very latest world, regional, and local news, and programs of interest for your listening pleasure, entertainment, and enlightenment.

"This is Art Zylstra, manager of radio station KICY, inviting you to remain tuned and reminding you of this bit of good news: 'Faith cometh by hearing and hearing by the word of God.' "

In order to clear his throat without being heard by his new listeners, Art flipped the microphone switch to the left momentarily. Then flipping it to the right again he introduced Howie Nelson, who proceeded to read yellow strips of paper torn from the Associated Press teletype machine. As Howie reported about a killer tornado in Oklahoma, China's political negotiations with neighboring Burma, and President Eisenhower's attendance at Easter services in Georgia, the noisy teletype machine could be heard clicking in the background.

On St. Lawrence Island, about 150 miles southwest of Nome, Dave and Mitzi Shinen, linguists with Wycliffe Bible Translators, heard that first broadcast. As they gathered in the Gambell Presbyterian Church after an Easter sunrise service on the beach, they noticed the village president had placed a battery-operated radio on a stand in front of the room. While

Art Zylstra at the microphone and Ralph Fondell in the control room of the KICY studio

the group ate seagull eggs and dried walrus, they listened to recordings of hymns and, for the first time ever, a weather forecast for St. Lawrence Island.

After that initial fifteen-minute report of world, national, and Alaskan news, Art switched over to Roald Amundsen, who was at the Nome high school with a remote transmitter unit to broadcast the annual Easter sunrise service featuring pastors from several area churches. Later that day, the KICY dedication ceremony, which had been taped three weeks earlier, was broadcast.

The day was exhilarating. The message of Easter's hope combined with the fulfillment of years of preparation and anticipation to create a fresh awareness of God's power to answer prayer and changes lives. After the station signed off at 11 p.m., the staff returned to their homes. They were exhausted, but excited as they thought of what God had in mind for the station in the days ahead.

The following day listeners got a taste of a typical day of broadcasting on KICY. The staff had spent countless hours attempting to discern the needs and wants of people in Nome and in the villages, and the log of programs reflected a diversity of flavors.

Following the early morning news was Wilbur Nelson's syndicated show "The Morning Chapel Hour." The show's theme song welcomed the day: "It is morning, the Son's in my heart, even when it's cloudy all day. It is morning, the shadows depart. Every day's a wonderful day." This was followed by more news, a community bulletin board program where listeners could promote club events or sell household items, and an hour-long program hosted by Art called "Musical Mailbag." A segment of Bible reading followed later in the morning. At noon there was a fifteen-minute segment called "Pause for Prayer" that preceded the midday news.

In the afternoon, Gert Fondell hosted a program for young homemakers challenged by the demands of young children, housework, and stressful marriages. Borrowing the title from a program aired at their previous station in Kentucky, Gert called the half-hour segment "Lines from a Mother's Scrapbook." It was followed by a talk show called "From a Woman's Point of View."

The balance of the afternoon included a fifteen-minute program produced by the Narramore Christian Foundation called "Psychology for

Living." This show, featuring Christian psychologist Clyde Narramore, dealt with finding solutions to life's problems. There were also children's programs from the Moody Broadcasting Network, including "Ranger Bill" and "Sailor Sam." "Back to the Bible," a twenty-five-minute Bible study produced by Good News Broadcasting Association, rounded out the afternoon schedule.

In May, the "Eskimo Hour" was introduced during the five o'clock hour. The show was hosted by Fred Savok, who had arrived in Nome that month to be associate pastor of the Nome church and director of Alaska Native programming for KICY. It quickly became one of KICY's most popular programs. Assisted by his wife, Gladys, and by Thomas Tungwenuk, a member of the Nome Covenant Church, Fred translated regional and national news into one of three Native dialects—Iñupiaq, Yupik, or Siberian Yupik. This news segment took up the first fifteen minutes of the program. The remaining thirty minutes of the forty-five-minute program was filled with pre-recorded hymns sung by village congregations in their specific dialect.

A variety of programs were offered in the evening hours until the 11 o'clock sign-off. News and music gave way to "Stories of Great Christians," a Moody program dramatizing the lives of well-known saints, and "Unshackled," a drama produced by the Pacific Garden Mission in Chicago. At 8 p.m. KICY introduced a fifteen-minute segment that would quickly become a signature program.

The "Ptarmigan Telegraph" (pronounced "tarmigan") invited listeners to call or write in messages for family members, work colleagues, or dis-

Fred Savok hosting the "Eskimo Hour"

tant relatives. These brief comments would then be read on the air so that the intended recipient would hear and respond in an appropriate manner. At the time home phone service was not available. Instead, each village might have one phone, usually a pay phone. Some of the larger towns, such as Nome, had privately owned phone exchanges, but communication was still very difficult. The "Ptarmigan Telegraph" soon became an indispensable lifeline to the area. It was a service unique to Alaska. The FCC forbade communicating private communiqués over public airwaves except in Alaska where villages were remote. Other stations in the state had similar programs, including "Caribou Clatter," "Tundra Topics," and "Mukluk Telegraph."

The "Ptarmigan Telegraph" announced all news that was "fit to broadcast." It announced when Uncle Jim would be arriving at fish camp or the fact that Doris had given birth to a healthy baby boy. It announced the arrival of a shipment of caribou meat on a chartered flight and it called for medical help for someone too sick to be transported. Dave Shinen, the Wycliffe translator on St. Lawrence Island, heard the news that his father in California had died.

Each day KICY gave seven updated news and weather reports. For the first time listeners had up-to-the minute forecasts and warnings of approaching storms, severe temperature drops, and low-pressure fronts moving in from the Bering Sea. In a part of the world that was accessible only by ship, plane, or dog sled, news of blinding storms, treacherous winds, and floating ice packs could save lives. KICY provided a vital service with these brief weather reports.

KICY's signal was heard in the original Covenant mission villages of Unalakleet, Golovin, White Mountain, and Elim. It was also reaching villages far beyond Norton Sound. Listeners were identified 300 or so miles south in the delta region of the Yukon and Kuskokwin Rivers as well to the north throughout the Seward Peninsula. In addition to St. Lawrence Island, the signal carried to both Little and Big Diomede Islands and Nunivak Island lodged in the frozen Bering Sea. A letter from the Russian government to the U.S. government protesting the existence of KICY gave the Covenant reason to believe the transmission from KICY's tower was reaching the people in Siberia who Axel Karlson had dreamed of reaching seventy-five years earlier.

For hundreds of uninterrupted miles, the new radio station was being heard loud and clear. With 5,000 watts of non-directional power, the potential listening audience was thought to exceed 40,000 people, two-thirds of whom were Alaska Natives. Within the first month the station received more than a thousand letters from eighty different villages.

One of the first letters was postmarked in Port Graham, 130 miles southwest of Anchorage. It read, "Just a note from a missionary not far from Seldovia. Be assured that I do enjoy your station. I thank God for it. It is so needed in this state."

Lily Savok, mother of Fred Savok, broadcasts the news for the "Eskimo Hour."

Another letter began, "A transistor fever has hit our Yukon village. Every adult owns a tiny radio. It is carried around as a lady carries her purse. An Eskimo building a rowboat outdoors listens to his radio operating full blast five feet away. A seal hunter has one with him in his boat. Even a woman cleaning fish props hers on the grass by her feet."

Still another letter was received from a biologist on a fisheries research vessel maneuvering through the Aleutian Islands. He wrote, "As you know, this is a bleak, desolate area and our joys are few (especially in stormy weather). One bright spot is KICY. . . ."

One letter in particular seemed to capture what hundreds of others said in one way or another: "It is very nice to have KICY station. I always listen every day. I sure proud to have your station KICY 'cause it sure makes me learn plenty of Christian ways. Also when I listen to your religious programs it sure makes me feel good and happy. . . ."

CHAPTER SEVEN

Fine Tuning the Mission

For the mushers who compete in the 1,100-mile trek of the Iditarod, a well-packed sled is as important as a well-trained team of dogs. Each sled is crammed with every imaginable resource that might be needed. A well-equipped musher will have packed a sleeping bag, a portable kerosene stove, an axe, and an assortment of other equipment for both anticipated needs and any unpredictable emergency. Tackling the trail means traveling with a full complement of devices that will cover all contingencies.

From KICY's beginning, general manager Art Zylstra recognized both its incredible opportunity to bring the gospel to listeners, and its civic responsibility to the communities they sought to serve. The daily programming log was a mix of news, sports, personal messages, prerecorded Christian ministry programs, and a wide assortment of music.

An article in the *Nome Nugget* that appeared when the station was launched summed it up best: "The 5,000 watt radio voice for Nome . . . is planning a schedule of varied programs that will be attractive to listeners with varying interests. Although the station receives it major support from a denominational source and its avowed primary purpose is the presentation of the 'good news' to be found in the Bible, this by no means signifies that all the programming will be religious in nature. In actual fact, only a small percentage of KICY's broadcast time will be devoted to religious programs.

"In conformity with the Federal Communications Commission, licensing requirements [mandate] that the station operate 'in the public interest, convenience, and necessity.' KICY will carry a 'balanced' schedule so arranged as to be informative, educational, entertaining, and inspiring. . . . A wide variety of music is included in the more than 1,000 long-play albums found in the KICY record library. The station will serve the musical interests that range all the way from the classics to country and western tunes, including band, pops concert, easy listening, and religious music. A good part of the broadcasting day will be devoted to music with some programs given over to selections which listeners request."

For Art, an ordained Covenant minister as well as a seasoned broadcaster, balanced programming was more than compliance with FCC guidelines. It was also a way of complying with the guidelines of the great commission. KICY's goal of reaching people with the good news of the gospel would only be achieved by following the Apostle Paul's commitment to become "all things to all people that by all possible means he might save some" (1 Corinthians 9:22). To gain a hearing for the gospel among listeners, programming must meet their needs and appeal to their interests.

An example of this occurred in 1961 when Alaska Natives were deprived, by the U.S. Fish and Wildlife Service under the Migratory Bird Act of 1918, of their right to subsistence hunt migratory waterfowl out of season. KICY solicited letters of opinion on the issue and forwarded them to Washington, D.C. after reading the letters over the air.

Early surveys estimated that of the 40,000 people within the listening area, 3,000 were tuning in to KICY at any given time during the day. It was an exciting time for both the new broadcast team as well as listeners.

After KICY had been on the air for two months, the staff welcomed two North Park College students from Chicago, Jim Engwall and Stan Summers, who wanted to spend their summer vacation contributing in anyway they could. "As I arrived in Nome I remember thinking how great it was to be in Alaska but also how far I was from home," Jim later recalled. "That summer I was a put to work doing a variety of tasks. But mostly I involved myself doing whatever needed to be done. I was impressed with how the station was impacting the community of Nome for Christ."

Both students quickly made themselves useful both on and off the air. From time to time they looked through the glass window in the studio door to watch Art Zylstra dwarf the control console each night as he would play records requested by listeners. KICY's daily musical fare was a little bit classical, a little bit gospel, and little bit polka, and a whole lot of country western, and listeners identified favorites in every genre. The most requested record that first summer was Burl Ives singing "Little White Duck."

Stan Summers
(left) and Jim
Engwall, volunteers
from North Park
College in the
summer of 1960

"It was really something to observe," Jim recalled. "So many people would call in that Art finally had to limit those requesting songs and encouraged them to send their requests by mail. That didn't bother too many listeners since phone service wasn't available in most villages. But even at that, there often were more than a hundred requests waiting at the post office."

Although the people of Nome and the eighty or so surrounding villages had listened to the Armed Forces station in Nome as well as picked up distant stations via shortwave, this was their first time they could interact with a disc jockey. Not only could they request a selection, they could dedicate it to someone. The DJ would announce both the requester's name and the dedication name on the air.

One elderly woman repeatedly called to request "How Great Thou Art" and dedicated it to Art Zylstra, whose voice she knew well but had never seen. She did not realize how appropriate her request was—not only was the much-loved hymn written by a Covenant pastor 100 years earlier in Sweden, the man to whom she dedicated it was "great" in both height and weight!

Letters sent to the station that summer confirmed that the "Eskimo Hour" was meeting an obvious need. One couple said that the broadcast meant so much to them that when they were out fishing, they would cut the outboard motor whenever the program started and just drift with the stream in order to hear everything on their transistor radio. A village pastor wrote to say that the program was so popular that evening services at church were regularly delayed so that members would not have to miss any of the "Eskimo Hour" before arriving for worship and prayer.

Fred and Gladys
Savok and family

The Savoks received a letter from a listener in the village of Perryville far to the south on the Alaska Peninsula. It was from a Christian who observed that every Friday the "Eskimo Hour" was in the dialect spoken by the older Aleuts in his village. For many it meant hearing the Bible in their own language for the first time. His letter asked if tapes of the broadcast could be purchased for broad distribution in the village. Within a short time the tapes were on their way.

One listener on Nunivak Island admitted that he'd avoided the Native broadcasts because they forced him to admit he was not a Christian and that left him feeling guilty. But the letter went on to describe his conversion. It ended with "I want to be a Christian like you are Fred."

In developing a collection of musical offerings, Fred and Gladys provided village churches with tape recorders to record gospel songs and hymns sung in the village's dialect. Often, these were the first tape recorders the churches had used. When Dave and Mitzi Shinen, the Wycliffe translators on St. Lawrence Island, moved to Nome so their children could attend school, they worked with Siberian Yupik believers to produce "Eskimo Hour" programs in that dialect.

The Savoks were the perfect couple to provide Jim Engwall and Stan Summers a delightful exposure to the unique joys of living in the northland. During the long summer evenings when the Arctic sun showed no indication of setting, Fred and Gladys introduced the Chicago volunteers to the thrill of picking wild blueberries, salmon berries, and yellow willow leaves. They told them where to plant a crab pot or cast a line for a king salmon. For both young men, a love for Nome was being planted.

In the fall of 1960, KICY expanded its programming to cover the popular local high-school basketball games. For a new station attempting to generate revenue from advertising sales, basketball season proved to be both a profitable time for the station and a favorite time of year for the listeners. Not everyone was enthusiastic about the station's play-by-play coverage of the games. Some questioned why a Christian station would broadcast local sports. But basketball represented more than athletic competition. The sports broadcasts provided wholesome entertainment in small towns lacking television, concerts, or movies, and which were often clouded by unemployment and alcohol abuse. KICY provided a community service and created good will by broadcasting the games.

KICY eventually extended its sports coverage. It introduced baseball to the area by carrying the World Series each fall through a network link. The station also introduced college football by broadcasting the weekly games of the University of Washington.

During that first winter of operation, concerns developed among the broader Covenant missionary community regarding the radio station's

Bessie Moss presents the news for the "Eskimo Hour" in the Iñupiaq dialect.

81

influence within the Covenant Missionary Council of Alaska. As missionaries commissioned by the Annual Meeting, the Fondells, Nelsons, and Zylstras felt they should be members of the council, along with the other commissioned missionaries. Some of the missionaries in the villages and at Covenant High School at Unalakleet felt that if all of the missionaries on staff at KICY were members of the council, the concerns of the radio station would dominate the vote on all issues, including those that did not pertain to broadcasting. They felt that one staff member should represent KICY.

Music for the "Eskimo Hour" was provided by village church singing groups.

Art Zylstra stood up for his staff. He believed they had every right to be heard on every issue, as the other members of the council did. After lengthy discussions, the Department of World Mission decided that the radio station staff called as missionaries would each have a voice on the council.

In the spring of 1961, health concerns and previous commitments to World Missionary Radio Fellowship led Art to end his term as general manager. He had moved his family to Nome with the understanding that their time there would most likely be relatively brief. He took the assignment to provide a successful launch of the station, and help establish its initial direction. In his 1961 annual report to the Covenant Annual Meeting, Ralph Hanson expressed his appreciation to Art for his dedication to the work while at the same time expressing concern that Art's tremendous contribution to KICY may have come at the expense of his health. The Zylstras returned to California, and after several months of rest, Art began raising funds and planning for a new World Missionary Radio Fellowship station in Montevideo, Uruguay.

Although Art's departure left a huge void at KICY, a qualified replacement was quickly found. Lloyd Sundstrom, manager of the White Alice Communications Project, a satellite relay system in Nome, had played a key role behind the scenes prior to KICY going on the air. His expertise in administration and knowledge of radio technology more than qualified him to step in to the vacant position at the station.

Lloyd inspired a renewed sense of purpose within the staff when he invited them to visualize the magnitude of the ministry in which they were involved. "Imagine an area extending 500 miles in every direction from where you are now located, with no connecting roads and only the airplane for basic transportation," he said pointing to the massive map of Alaska in the manager's office. "Radio is one of the best methods of mass communication. From one centrally located installation we are able to communicate with almost all the people in this area. God has given us a wonderful and extremely powerful tool to bring his word to everyone who will listen. It knows no bounds!"

Jim Engwall returned to Nome in the summer of 1961 to spend another vacation volunteering at the station. He met up with an engineering student from the University of Minnesota named Earl "Chip" Swanson. Chip jumped right in. With a love for the wilderness and camping, Chip took full advantage of learning the operation of the station and the trails that led out of town. The work of these college students continued a pattern of invaluable volunteer involvement that began in the months leading up to the station's debut, and which has continued to today. In addition to full-time staff that provided stability and vision, there

Chip Swanson
in the summer
of 1961

was a need for those who would be willing to provide their own transportation and support to supplement the operation.

In the fall, when the students had returned to the lower forty-eight, another full-time couple arrived. Ernie Hansen, a Covenant pastor, and his wife, Barbara, came from California with a particular sense of call. Nonbelievers who regularly listened to the sports, news, or the "Ptarmigan Telegraph" did not necessarily turn off their radios when these programs were over. Many were intrigued by hearing God's word in their birth language for the first time on the "Eskimo Hour." Others were drawn in by one of the radio dramas with a Christian message. But how could the station respond to their spiritual curiosity? Who would follow up and send out materials or be available to provide spiritual counsel? Ernie and Barbara made themselves available to take on that challenge.

Ernie and Barbara Hansen and family arrived in Nome in 1961.

Very quickly the Hansens identified other challenges facing the fledgling station. Despite the generosity of Covenanters and the enthusiasm for the project, estimates of operation costs were unrealistically low. The cost of purchasing and maintaining equipment in a very isolated environment was greater than expected. The Hansens realized that the station needed to make sure that the rest of the Covenant Church knew the wonderful things that were happening in Nome, and its need for financial support, although the policies surrounding the Covenant's unified budgeting system limited fund-raising to specific projects and did not allow KICY to solicit Covenant individuals and churches to support the operating budget of the station.

Shortly after finding a rhythm to his new ministry, Ernie heard a fur trader tell how influential KICY was throughout the region. According to this man, whatever people in bush Alaska heard on KICY they believed. This news at once thrilled the new radio minister but also caused him to consider the responsibility he and other staffers had to make sure they were being faithful to God's call. Within a few months Ernie was editing the station's monthly prayer letter that was sent throughout the rest of the U.S. and Canada to churches and individuals who had expressed interest in the ministry of KICY. The monthly communiqué was aptly called the "KICY Call Letter."

The letter kept the broader church informed on the goings on in Nome and at the radio station. When Will Rogers Jr. stopped by, it was reported in the "Call Letter." The same was true when legendary CBS news reporter Lowell Thomas paid the station a visit. But the "Call Letter" served a much more practical purpose. Biographical summaries of new staff members were included. Letters from listeners were excerpted. Fundraising projects were identified. But primarily, readers of the "Call Letter" were asked to pray for specific concerns.

Another challenge the Hansens encountered was the demands a seventeen-hour broadcast day had put on a small staff. Staff worked almost around the clock developing and producing programming. These tasks, coupled with the need to sell and produce advertisement, resulted in an overworked, exhausted staff. There were no designated days off and the deep commitment that the staff had to the mission led them to put the good of the station ahead of their own well-being. Ernie understood the need to care for the staff, and within six months of his arrival he had arranged for each staff person to have a half day off each week and one Sunday a month.

By the spring of 1962, Lloyd Sundstom and his wife, Vesta, decided they had contributed as much as they could to the stabilization of the new station. Ernie Hansen, who had joined the staff eight months earlier, was chosen as the new general manager. Admitting his lack of experience, Ernie accepted the new challenge, asking his colleagues and daily KICY listeners to pray for him.

The team was strengthened in October 1962 with the arrival of Donald and Eunice Bruckner. As the leadership roles shifted, Don was able to assist the staff in a variety of ways, as interim news director, announcer, and assistant engineer. He produced "The Old Log Cabin," a program in which he interviewed local elders and old timers about the days past in Nome. In the summer of 1963 he oversaw the construction of an additional house for KICY staff. Eunice, a registered nurse working at the local hospital, gave her salary to the mission, and produced a program on home health tips and nutrition.

Howie and Pat Nelson departed in the spring of 1963, but under Ernie Hansen's leadership, KICY continued to flourish. The Fondells, Bruckners, and Savoks joined with Ernie and Barbara to constantly evaluate the station's work and address its needs.

In the summer of 1963 another full-time staffer was added to the team. Chip Swanson had been inspired by his summer experience two years earlier. Having just graduated with his degree in electrical engineering, Chip couldn't think of any place he would rather practice his knowledge than at the 5,000-watt station on the coast of the Bering Sea. Taking on the early morning announcer shift, Chip soon won the hearts of listeners in village after village. His humor and optimism provided the spark on which Christians and non-Christians alike grew to depend as they began their daily routines. One of the most popular features on Chip's early morning program was the "riddle machine" where he would invite people to call in the answer to the daily riddle.

But not all developments in Nome in 1963 were good. That year, driven by the price of gold in world markets, the Alaska Gold Company shut down the majority of its mining operation. Because AGC was the major employer in Nome, this decision left a dark shadow over the treeless landscape of Norton Sound.

The town's longtime mayor, Leo Rasmussen, has praised KICY as being

Margaret Zylstra leads the Sunshine Club in 1961.

a major player in the emotional recovery of a town that forty years later is still rebounding from the layoffs. As far as he was concerned, the Christian station helped the teetering community maintain a sense of balance by providing a radiant message. "What is more," he added, "the investment that KICY's staff members and their families made in the community can't be underestimated."

From the beginning, the staff at KICY tried to serve the community as a whole. Art Zylstra hosted an on-air Bible club for kids called the Sunshine Club. The show aired on Saturday mornings, and while at first only the missionary children and their friends came, soon the KICY studio was packed with close to ninety children. The children loved being on the radio and they enjoyed spending time with "Uncle Art." Margaret Zylstra, who played music for the show, and a volunteer named Erma Johnson decided it was a shame to have the children for such a short time each Saturday, so they expanded the Sunshine Club for an additional forty-five minutes after the show went off the air each Saturday.

Children from the Sunshine Club gather outside the KICY studio.

And not all outreach centered around the station. Margaret Zylstra and Grace Johnson, capitalizing on Art's good reputation in Nome, received permission from the warden at the Nome jail to hold Bible studies with women who were incarcerated. As other staff served on the PTA, in Boy Scouts, Chamber of Commerce, Rotary, Board of Education, and the City Council, KICY became more than the church-owned station on the corner of 4th and D Streets. It increasingly was viewed as Nome's radio station.

By building friendships and investing in the life of the community, the staff won the hearts of those to whom they attempted to minister. That reality was poignantly demonstrated when the Fondells returned from a several-month furlough in the lower forty-eight. On the day the family, which had by now grown to seven, was returning, the KICY staff piled into two vehicles and headed to the Nome airport to greet them. Ruthie Towner, a leading citizen of Nome, walked the two miles to the airport flanked by a pack of young children who loved Ralph and Gert. Barbara Hansen recalled the tender scene she witnessed when the Fondells finally arrived.

"I struck up a conversation with a tourist from Beverly Hills waiting for her flight. Having seen Nome she was very curious about what had drawn us to live there. Then when the plane carrying the Fondells landed she watched all the little kids hanging on the chain link fence yelling and laughing, excited about the return of their friends. That was followed by lots of hugging as Ralph and Gert and their children reached the terminal. When we left the airport, the woman from Beverly Hills, who was used to seeing Hollywood celebrities shadowed, stopped me and with tears in her eyes said, 'That is the most beautiful thing I have ever seen.'"

While the community of Nome was drawn together through the contributions made by the station's personnel, the staff was being drawn together as a community within the community. The staff worked together, worshiped together, and played together. Although all but the Savoks were thousands of miles away from their extended families, their coworkers had become as close as brothers and sisters.

The draw of the KICY community was strong. In the summer of 1964, Art Zylstra returned for a summer. He was recovering from a heart attack the previous spring and he wanted to spend his recovery doing something he loved in a stress-free environment. The now slimmed-down Art was pleased with the progress the station had made in the three years since he had left. Art even had the opportunity to go to the village of Kotzebue, north of Nome, to relate the story of KICY. For the better part an hour, Art, a gifted storyteller, captivated his audience with the miracles that surrounded the starting of KICY. Tragically, this would be the last time Art would tell the story of KICY. Days later, while flying over the Sierra Mountains on his way back to Chicago, he died of a massive heart attack. He was forty-three years old.

One cannot overestimate the contribution Art Zylstra made in getting KICY started and in laying the foundation for its long-term success. In 1945 the Covenant had decided not to move forward with plans for a radio station in Alaska, in part because they did not feel they had a person qualified to lead the station. In 1958, with Art agreeing to lead the project, the Covenant decided it was time to start a radio ministry in Alaska. Art's passion to use radio as a tool to tell the gospel message left an indelible mark on KICY. Forty years after his death, the words he spoke in that church in Kotzebue still influence those who work at KICY today. As a part of their orientation, new volunteers and staff listen to an audiotape of that message.

Competition, Expansion, Crisis

Every Iditarod sled dog race since the first in 1973 has included unanticipated challenges that take a personal toll and require creative responses. Sometimes it is injury to a lead dog that requires one of the other fifteen to leap frog to the front and discover an unobstructed view. Sometimes there is damage to a sled or a musher becomes ill. Sometimes a treacherous blizzard grounds the team for hours.

In 2003, it wasn't blizzard conditions but a lack of snow in the Anchorage basin that created a challenge. That year it was warmer in Alaska than in many parts of the American Midwest. Snow was trucked in for the ceremonial beginning to the race. The actual start of that year's Iditarod was moved to Fairbanks, 350 miles to the north, and the itinerary of the course had to be substantially revised. Not only was there a lack of snow on the normal trail, the mushers could not race on the Yukon River because it was not sufficiently frozen. Although traditionalists were disappointed, there was some consolation. For the first time in the history of the race, mushers followed a route similar to the 1925 serum run.

Of the original three couples, the Fondells, the Zylstras, and the Nelsons, called by the Covenant to establish KICY, only one was in Nome to celebrate the station's tenth anniversary in 1970. Ralph and Gert Fondell remained deeply rooted in the work that drew them to Alaska, and had established meaningful connections in the community.

Stan Summers returned to KICY in 1965, but this time it wasn't just for the summer as it had been the previous years. Newly married, Stan and Beth Summers were commissioned as missionaries at the 1965 Covenant Annual Meeting and joined the KICY staff. They soon discovered the bonding that the others had come to cherish. So did Dave and Kathy DeVries, who were commissioned as missionaries at the 1967 Covenant Annual Meeting and moved to Nome that fall. This newlywed couple from Willmar, Minnesota, spent the summers of 1965 and 1966 at KICY as a way of testing the water for a long-term commitment. The strong sense of family more than compensated for the challenges they knew they would face in such a remote location.

Stan and Beth
Summers and
daughter Jennifer

"When you are separated from what is familiar and cherished in a remote place where you have to fend for yourselves, you discover that you suddenly have something in common with those around you," Kathy said, describing the relationships they formed with their station colleagues. "The emotional bonds you build with those who are dealing with the same issues of homesickness and insecurity are lifelong."

It was also in 1967 that Don and Eunice Bruckner moved to Fairbanks and Don began working for Alaska Airlines. Ernie and Barbara Hansen moved to San Jose, California, where Ernie served as the pastor of Alum

Rock Covenant Church. Ernie's replacement as manager was Ralph Fondell, who had handled the station's engineering responsibilities from the beginning. Looking back his the wide variety of broadcasting experience, he saw God's hand preparing him for "such a time as this." Chip Swanson took over as chief engineer.

Dave and Kathy
DeVries

Each of the staff had their own responsibilities, which included hosting call-in request shows, ripping off the Associated Press teletype pages and reading news headlines, compiling the "Ptarmigan Telegraph" messages, answering the phone, and reviewing the records that would be played during Chip's popular morning show. Kathy DeVries enjoyed sorting through vinyl albums that record companies sent to the station. She earned the nickname "The Great Taper" because of the frequency with which she would place Scotch tape over a particular song whose lyrics were inappropriate for a Christian station to play.

The neighborhood in which the staff lived was colorfully unique. Because each of the homes was painted with different paint, the color became the point of reference in distinguishing them. Most everyone in town knew that the Fondells lived in the brown house, the DeVries lived in the gray house, and the Summers lived in the blue house. The red house was often used for volunteers who came to help out for a short time. The yellow house had been the home of past station managers, but since the Fondells were settled in their own home, the yellow house next door to the studio building remained vacant.

As word about the new radio station spread throughout the Covenant denomination, interested pastors and church leaders wanted a chance to check out the broadcast ministry for themselves. On countless occasions

Dave and Kathy would host them. Not only was the layout of the two-story gray house well-suited for hosting guests, the young couple loved to entertain. Kathy took delight in giving their visitors a taste of Alaska's gold rush glory. On the day they departed she would surprise them with homemade sourdough pancakes. (Kathy acquired the sourdough starter as a gift when she and Dave came as volunteers in the summer of 1965. Forty years later, she is still using it to make Alaska pancakes for guests she entertains at Covenant Harbor Bible Camp in Wisconsin.)

In the fall of 1971 Jim and Lola Engwall and their twin boys arrived and took up residence in the yellow house. Ever since the summer of 1962, when Jim had worked at KICY as a student volunteer, he had dreamed of one day returning. Now with experience as a hospital administrator, Jim had realized his dream. He assumed the role of business manager and news director while Lola handled bookkeeping responsibilities.

Jim and Lola
Engwall

For an extrovert like Jim, his dual position suited him well. He became friends with the local merchants he approached with advertising opportunities. As he drank coffee with the regulars at the Polar Cub Café on Front Street, he not only got leads on stories for the daily newscasts, he found himself counseling those dealing with personal problems. Jim's skill in investigating news stories and reporting them gained him a reputation as a skilled journalist. Jim was twice asked to fill-in for nationally known reporter Charles Kuralt on his "Dateline America" radio program, when Kuralt's other reporting duties at CBS kept him away.

While Jim worked within the community, Lola ministered to the staff. Her positive personality and sense of humor kept those at the station laughing on days when unmet deadlines or ugly weather had them on the brink of tears. On dark days in December when daylight was not longer than four hours, Lola's sunny smile and dry wit went a long way to keep her colleagues from going stir crazy.

Stan Summers's job as program director was also a critical one. The choices he made determining what programs and music should be played and when they would be aired, shaped the personality of the station. He had to think through the entire day of broadcasting and evaluate it from the various needs of an extremely wide spectrum of listeners. It was Stan's job to balance serving the community (including making a positive impression on non-Christian listeners) and maintaining Christian standards.

Although KICY was committed to excellence in everything it did, the realities of a small station in a remote part Alaska with limited resources meant that productions were not always as polished as the staff had planned. At such times, Beth Summers recalled what someone had said when she was about to move to Alaska. A friend had told her not to be overly concerned with the run-down exterior of the homes she would see in Nome. What really mattered were the good-hearted people who lived behind those less-than-perfect facades. Beth discovered the wisdom of those words soon enough. She came to realize that what was true of the houses was also true of a station whose occasional not-so-perfect programming did not detract from the sincerity and hard work of those who were doing their best.

The best KICY could do one summer required ingenuity and a willingness to think—and work—outside the box. When a dump truck out near the transmitter site accidentally severed the station's radio cable, the signal disappeared. Until the cable could be repaired, Dave, Stan, and Ralph jimmy-rigged a makeshift solution. They set up a portable studio on the beach southeast of town. There, in the open air, Dave broadcast news and spun records for the benefit of Nome residents as well as the gulls perched on nearby driftwood. While swatting mosquitoes and shielding the microphone from the constant wind, Dave transformed a less-than-ideal set of circumstances into an unforgettable memory.

KICY's attempts to present balanced programming that met the needs of both Christians and non-Christians were successful. Nome and the surrounding villages expressed appreciation for the way KICY was able to entertain, inspire, and provide information related to the outside world, incoming weather, scheduled (and unscheduled) flights, as well as personal messages.

An unexpected newcomer to Nome succeeded in throwing the staff off balance, however. In the summer of 1971, a few months before the Engwalls arrived, a new radio station came to town.

The Roman Catholic mission in western Alaska had grown increasingly uncomfortable with KICY's programming. Although it did not object to the valuable service KICY provided with its news, weather, and sports coverage, it was concerned that the Christian teaching was not meeting a Catholic need, and was drawing people away from the Catholic Church.

Relocating to Nome from the Yukon Delta in the mid-sixties, Father Jim Poole committed himself to building a radio station that would serve Catholics in the region. After a number of setbacks, he finally succeeded. Nome's second radio station, KNOM, went on the air on July 14, 1971.

One major distinction between the two stations was that KNOM was not licensed as a commercial station and therefore could not sell advertising. They were solely dependent on donations. Other than that, KNOM mirrored much of KICY's programming, with the exception of the obvious differences in religious broadcasts.

As KNOM went on the air, KICY discovered the mixed blessing of living with competition. The presence of KNOM made the KICY staff look at its mission and evaluate how effective they were in achieving that mission. As a result, the staff worked harder to live up to its mission and maintain the allegiance of listeners.

By 1973, KICY moved ahead with a new dimension to its programming, and began a Russian language broadcast. Since his seminary days at North Park when he wrote a term paper on "Missions in Alaska," Ralph Fondell had dreamed of the day a Covenant radio station could capitalize on Alaska's close proximity to the Soviet Union. It was the possibility of one day broadcasting to Russian-speaking people beyond the Bering Sea that energized him during the winter of 1959 before KICY had gone on the air. Five years later, in July 1964, Peter Deyneka Sr., a Russian immigrant and founder of the Slavic Gospel Association, visited Nome and conducted a brief crusade over KICY. It was aimed at those living in western Alaska who spoke Russian and those who might be able to pick up the broadcast across the Bering Strait. The impact of the radio crusade was memorable. It began to stir the embers in Ralph's heart with regard to Russia's back door. But since KICY's license from the FCC had not assumed international broadcasting, Ralph was concerned that the agency would not give approval to broadcast in Russian. After much consideration, Ralph suggested that Arctic Broadcasting Association (ABA), the holder of KICY's FCC license, apply to the FCC for permission to broadcast in Russian. The stated rationale for obtaining the license was to enable the station to provide programming for Russian-speaking Alaska Natives. Given the political chill of the Cold War, Ralph feared that a straightforward request to broadcast in Russian with a signal beamed toward Siberia would be buried in bureaucracy or denied.

Peter Deyneka,
founder of Slavic
Gospel Association,
spoke on KICY
in July 1964.

Within several months, the FCC granted the station permission to transmit programs in Russian. KICY now could broadcast in Russian as far as their signal carried, which was far beyond the few Russian-speaking Alaska Natives. Fully acknowledging that he didn't know anything about their intended Russian audience, Ralph went looking for teaching programs that had been produced by U.S.-based Russian evangelical ministries. This search proved profitable, as he contacted the Slavic Gospel Association, the Mennonite Broadcasts Inc., the Southern Baptist Convention, the Lutheran Church–Missouri Synod, and the Russian Gospel Temple in San Francisco.

By the spring of 1973 KICY was broadcasting Christian programs in Russian. The broadcasts were aired each evening from 11:00 to 11:30

p.m., the last thirty minutes prior to sign off. Although the majority of KICY listeners tuned out, countless others tuned in just for that precious half hour. Besides the Russian-speaking people in Alaska, the staff regularly prayed for those as yet unidentified listeners in the Soviet Far East with radios. Andrew Semenchuk, a missionary with Slavic Gospel Association, had given them reason to think that the audience could be extensive. He had recently visited Siberia. He said that the people he met scanned their radio dials in hopes of finding something other than Radio Moscow.

Dave Shinen, who was now back in Gambell on St. Lawrence Island, also gave the KICY staff reason to think the Russian broadcasts were being heard beyond Alaska. The residents of Gambell had relatives thirty-five miles to the west in Siberia and were in contact with them through short-wave radios. They indicated that KICY was being heard loud and clear.

Because of political constraints, listeners in the Soviet Union were not able to write directly to the American station. Still, the staff wanted to find a way to determine what kind of an impact the broadcasts were having. KICY sought the assistance of Covenanters in Sweden who opened up a post-office box in the station's name in Stockholm. As a result, listeners could write to an address in a neutral country. Hearing the Swedish address at the conclusion of the nightly broadcasts, those appreciating the ministry of KICY in their language began to express their gratitude by mail.

That same spring another local development sparked great interest among those living in and around Nome. A sled dog race more than 1,000 miles long from Anchorage to Nome had been talked about for years. In March 1973 it finally became a reality. The purpose was threefold. In an era when snow machines, commonly referred to as snowmobiles in the lower forty-eight, had become popular, Alaskans wanted to keep the romance of dog teams alive. They also wanted to honor the memory of the 1925 serum run that had saved the lives of hundreds of children in Nome during a diphtheria epidemic. Third, they wanted to generate a boost in the state's economy by creating a race that would draw competitors as well as tourists. Because a portion of the race would be run on the legendary Iditarod Trail, the race was named after it. And because the race would end in Nome, it was only natural that KICY would be involved in covering it. After all, the staff had covered the annual Northwest Alaska Championship Dog Race since the early sixties.

Dave DeVries, microphone in hand and bundled in his down parka, provided running commentary for KICY listeners as thirty-six dog teams competed for a first prize of $50,000. When Richard Wilmarth, the winning musher, directed his team down snow-covered Front Street, Dave reported the details so that those ice fishing on the Bering Sea or those sitting with a cup of hot coffee at home felt like they were in Nome. Unlike the crowd of thousands that would gather at the race's end thirty years later, only a small crowd of merchants and residents stood beside Dave that first year.

Jim Engwall interviews Iditarod musher Emmitt Peters.

In contrast to the media hype that the Iditarod would generate over the next three decades, the very first "Last Great Race" was not covered by CNN or *Wide World of Sports* or the Outdoor Network. Only KICY, KNOM, and the *Nome Nugget* were on hand. KICY did distinguish itself however that first year. Ever the assertive news reporter, Jim Engwall called in the results of the race to CBS radio in New York and they aired his report to every state in the country.

By the second year, however, the KICY staff determined that they could do a more complete job. In 1974, before the time of satellites, KICY pioneered the first extensive Iditarod coverage using a number of VHF remote units to broadcast live from all their vehicles. That included coverage from the last checkpoint at Safety (twenty-two miles east of Nome), to chartered airplanes flying over White Mountain (second to last checkpoint), to the reporter at the Front Street finish line.

Jim Engwall recalled the staff's ingenuity in pulling it off: "We had purchased some old tube-type VHF two-way radios, licensed them as broadcast remote VHF units, and installed two in our station vehicles, one in an airplane, and one on a sled pulled by a snowmobile. The airplane flew anywhere we needed coverage, the sled was pulled to Safety checkpoint where then KICY chief engineer Chip Swanson camped out with the Iditarod checker for about a week, and the station vehicles each served as mobile units."

During this time of expanded programming and creative coverage at the station, the Board of World Mission determined that the missionary enterprise in Alaska should no longer be under the supervision of a department that defined its parameters by foreign borders. As a result, the mission work in Alaska came under the umbrella of the Board of Home Mission in 1972, and KICY followed in 1973.

Many on the KICY staff did not agree with shift. For them the challenges of cross-cultural barriers into the world of the Alaska Natives was still on a level more consistent with a foreign mission than a home mission. Still, the decision by the denomination was consistent with the desire expressed by L. E. Ost back in 1919 that Alaska Natives take on the responsibility for the mission in Alaska, and that decisions that affected Alaska needed to be made by Alaskans. In order to achieve that objective, the Mission Council was replaced by the Evangelical Covenant Church of Alaska (ECCAK), which acted as the field office overseeing the work of the Covenant in Alaska. Decision-making was shifted from the denomination to the local churches in Alaska that acted through an annual meeting in which delegates from local churches met to transact business. In between annual meetings, the ECCAK Leadership Council, comprised of pastors and laypersons from local churches, transacted business that could not wait until the next meeting.

Home Mission sought to bring the ministries in Alaska into conformity with the Covenant's other work in the U.S. and Canada, which meant that these ministries needed to become financially self-sufficient. This would have a dramatic affect on KICY's funding. During the transition the denomination pledged financial help to the Alaska radio ministry. This annual appropriation eased the amount of money that would otherwise have to be generated by advertising sales or unsolicited contributions from churches and individuals. But the time was coming when financial assistance to KICY would no longer be included in Home Mission's budget.

Through it all, KICY remained committed to voicing a Christian witness. In addition to serving listeners with requested music, up-to-the-hour newscasts, sports coverage, and personal messages, the Bible teaching programs for adults, and Christian story programs for children remained a mainstay of the daily programming. Short evangelistic hooks called "God Spots" also served to remind listeners where the station was coming from. Members of the staff took turns writing and recording these sixty-second public service announcements that addressed a need in the lives of the people in the villages or in Nome and then invited them to look to God.

Despite KICY's expanded programming and staff stability, KNOM continued to win the allegiance of listeners who had once been committed to KICY. Concerned that the trend might continue, the staff decided to conduct an audience survey. Instead of playing an assortment of music (including sacred, gospel, classical, country, and pop), they wondered if they should develop a unique format driven by one particular musical style. Ralph asked long-time KICY supporter Bill Hartman for a recommendation to develop the survey. Bill introduced him to William "Ted" Haney of the Far East Broadcasting Company. Ted had vast experience in conducting listener surveys for the large radio missionary organization.

In the winter of 1976, Ted flew up and spent a couple weeks with the staff to find out what they wanted to learn from the survey. He then designed a questionnaire to identify what listeners wanted and needed.

William "Ted" Haney, executive director of Far East Broadcasting Company and long-time president of the Arctic Broadcasting Association board of directors

He hired a photographer to take aerial photographs of Nome and twenty-five villages. The photos made graphing possible from which random locations could be identified to conduct personal interview surveys.

"Looking back on the audience survey a couple things cause me to smile," Ted later observed. "One home identified from the air and earmarked for a visit turned out to be an abandoned car. And one person that was interviewed was so bundled in winter clothes it was impossible for the interviewer to indicate whether the person was male or female."

The survey, which took several months to complete, found that listeners preferred country western music. This was not entirely unexpected. Records by country artists like Chet Atkins, Hank Williams, and Johnny Cash were favorites on the daily request program. It was the kind of music the Armed Forces radio station had played in the 1940s and 1950s. Since many of the soldiers were from the South, it gave them a longed-for taste of home. And since the villagers could only pick up the military station prior to KICY, they developed a taste for that kind of music. In addition, there were similarities between Alaska Native music and country western music. Both styles tell stories and have their roots in a folk tradition.

While Ted's recommendation was in keeping with the ideas of the staff, Stan Summers and the rest of the staff were not as familiar with country music. As program director, Stan made a decision to modify the music format so that it was predominantly country music, but he also retained a mix of classical, popular, religious, and easy-listening music.

The survey also found that KICY had two different audiences—the tastes and interests of those living in Nome were different from those in the villages. The ABA board of directors responded by seeking a license that would enable KICY to operate a low power stereo FM signal that would be heard only in town in addition to the 5,000-watt AM signal that was heard in the villages. This would allow the station to target its programming to the two audiences. The request was quickly approved by the FCC and the station received a $30,000 gift from the American Lutheran Church earmarked for the FM project. With plans to blend instrumental orchestrations of popular music with instrumental sacred selections, KICY–FM went on the air September 11, 1977. The localized reception also allowed the station to serve the community by broadcasting Nome City Council meetings each week along with a call-in show allowing Nome residents to share their feelings about issues around town. Because the new FM station was primarily automated—operated by computer prompts that engaged lengthy pre-recorded music tapes—additional personnel were not needed to handle the increased programming. Ironically, it was at this time that Chip Swanson decided that fifteen years as an on-the-air personality and chief engineer were enough. Having reported the news from behind a microphone in the control room, Chip felt called to preach the good news from a pulpit. In 1977 he left to serve as the pastor in both the White Mountain and Golovin churches. Terry Reynolds, who had served as a volunteer five years earlier, moved to Nome with his wife, Linda, to take over as engineer.

In 1978 Yuri Ryetkhue, a Russian author and vice-president of the Soviet Writers' Union from Leningrad, visited Nome. He had been raised in eastern Siberia. During a broadcast interview with Ralph Fondell,

Terry and Linda Reynolds with daughter Sarah

Ryetkhue brought welcome news to the station. He had recently visited his home area and had heard KICY's programs. Up to this point, there had been numerous reports of Siberian listeners, including letters from listeners sent to the Stockholm address, but his report was the first confirmation delivered in person.

Ryetkhue's visit energized the station. Now approaching its twentieth anniversary, KICY sought to strengthen its signal and increase its coverage. The ABA board began the appropriate process with the FCC to increase KICY–AM from 5,000 watts to 10,000 watts. The station secured a grant from the Epaphroditus Foundation guaranteeing $30,000 over a five-year period. The Covenant Department of Christian Education raised more than $13,000 through the donations of children attending vacation

Bible schools. When the eventual approval came from the FCC, the balance of the $50,000 needed for the power boost trickled in. On July 24, 1980, KICY doubled its signal.

Although the station had raised the money for the expanded signal, rising operation costs resulted in the station accruing debt at a rate that was causing concern to Ralph and the board members of ABA. To make matters worse, it was becoming more and more difficult to secure volunteers who would stay more than one year.

Creative attempts at increasing revenue were explored. One such innovative approach was known as "Action Branch." The premise of this idea was simple. Not everyone who wanted to support the unique ministry of KICY with their labor had the necessary skills. Through the Action Branch program, people with other skills, such as nursing or teaching, could move to Nome for a year or more and work for the community hospital or a public school and then donate their salary to KICY. There was a precedent for the program. When Howie and Pat Nelson arrived in the fall of 1959, Howie had broadcasting experience and worked at the station, while Pat worked as a nurse at the Nome hospital. Because they were compensated as career missionaries, Pat was required by a policy of the Board of Missions to donate her income to the KICY budget. With the switch to the Board of Home Mission this policy was no longer in effect.

Deanna Johnson, a nurse from Duluth, Minnesota, was one of those who signed up for the Action Branch program. After attending the Urbana Missionary Conference at the University of Illinois, she decided she wanted to work in a cross-cultural setting. A member of her church encouraged her to contact KICY. In September 1985 she moved into the yellow house and worked at the North Sound Community Hospital. Her first two years she donated her entire salary to the station and in exchange she received housing and a stipend for living expenses. For the two years following that, she donated half her salary to the station. In her free time she worked at the station, producing the "Call Letter" and hosting a weekly classical music program. Deanna even met her future husband, Will Nelson, who was a bush airline pilot living in the apartment above the KICY station.

Even with people like Deanna responding to the call to join the Action

Branch, the station continued to struggle financially. But this was not the only concern. Informal surveys and staff visits to the villages were confirming a growing suspicion Ralph hoped was wrong. More and more people were listening to KNOM rather than KICY. This left the staff to question whether they were accomplishing the mission of KICY, to connect people in western Alaska and to share the good news of the gospel. A reduced listenership also affected their ability to sell advertising, which in turn affected the station's bottom line.

Although the reasons varied, one indicated that KNOM seemed to be more in touch with the needs of the Alaska Natives. Although KICY offered the "Eskimo Hour" each evening as well as "Music of the Northland," their overall sound was more attuned to a non-Native audience. Ralph recognized that this was due in part to the syndicated Christian programs like "Focus on the Family" and "Insight for Living." There were also comments that suggested that even the evangelicals in the villages were less loyal to KICY than in years past. Allegedly this was due to a lack of communication between the staff at KICY and the pastors of the village churches.

Ralph reluctantly admitted this was probably true. Beginning with the Engwalls in 1980, the full-time staff families had begun to leave Nome. The DeVries had left in 1982 and the Summers had left in 1984. There wasn't the employee base to maintain contact with the pastors as there once had been. The short-term volunteers who replaced the permanent staff didn't have the same rapport or time to invest in longstanding relationships.

As contact with the pastors and Christian leaders in the villages decreased, complaints about the station's format increased. Comments that questioned KICY's Christian commitment (because only 25 percent of the programming was overtly Christian in content) illustrated the lack of ongoing communication. That had been the percentage of Christian programming from the very beginning. But without the staff's ability to explain the station's mission, faulty assertions could not be answered or challenged. But the issues were more complex than a lack of communication. An explosion in media options had also occurred.

An increasing number of people were turning off their radios and watching television in their homes. Cable access television and satellite dishes radically changed the landscape of western Alaska. Starting in the mid-seventies the news and entertainment needs KICY had once solely provided, could now be accessed through satellite television. By the mid-eighties VCRs were readily available and created another entertainment option that competed with KICY.

Since the station had gone on the air in 1960, the annual cost of operating KICY had jumped from $50,000 to $225,000 by 1980. Unfortunately, advertising sales and direct contributions had never approached the actual costs. Gifts from churches and individuals made up the differences, but Covenant policies limited KICY's ability to raise funds to offset operating expenses. Further compounding the problems was the implementation in 1979 of a policy by the Board of Home Mission that called for upper limits on the amount of appropriation support for the Covenant's work in Alaska. The goal of the policy was to move churches and institutions towards being self-sufficient. For KICY this meant that annual appropriations from the denomination were to go from $85,000 in 1980 down to $50,000 in 1984 and stop thereafter.

The ABA board could see the handwriting on the wall. Something drastic needed to happen. They responded with two initiatives. First, they encouraged Ralph and Gert Fondell to leave Nome and launch two sister stations in Anchorage and Bethel. Although there would be increased debt to start the stations, they believed the primary administrative positions (which was the biggest cost to KICY) could be shared by all three stations. While the stations generated advertising revenue, their overhead costs would be drastically reduced. After twenty-five years, Ralph was ready for a change in location and was willing to take on the challenge.

The second initiative was suggested by Bill Hartman, who after years of service to KICY had remained on the ABA board. He agreed to lobby the denomination with a proposal whereby KICY would be able to solicit funds directly from any of the almost 600 Covenant churches. In this proposal, Bill argued that non-Covenant ministries were not under the same restrictions of the Covenant's unified budgetary system and therefore these ministries had a distinct advantage over the Covenant's own ministries, such as KICY. The Hartman Proposal recommended a significant departure from Covenant policy and it was debated extensively by the Executive Board of the Covenant, before being recommended for and receiving approval at the 1985 Annual Meeting.

Whereas the Hartman Proposal would prove successful in helping KICY to increase the financial support they received from churches and individuals, the concept of an ABA radio network with KICY as the flag-ship station would fail. Nonetheless, in spite of problems that would continue to plague the financially stricken station, there appeared to be adequate reasons to believe it was too soon to give up.

CHAPTER NINE

Making Adjustments without Changing Direction

The mushers who participated in the first Iditarod in 1973 were concerned with finishing the race not strategy. The goal was to survive the course no matter how long it took. Whereas Richard Wilmarth of Red Devil, Alaska, finished the 1,100 miles in twenty days in 1973, in 1995 Doug Swingley of Simms, Montana, proved it could be done in half the time. He completed the icy course in just over nine days.

With each successive year, mushers looked for ways to trim time from the grueling trek. They bred faster dogs and strategized where to rest their team and themselves. Some mushers exchanged their heavy-duty sled for a lightweight racing sled once they reached the Safety Roadhouse twenty-two miles outside Nome. Without the need for excess food or gear, mushers can get along with a smaller sled. The end result is the ability to travel the final leg of the journey at a faster rate of speed across the frozen Bering Sea.

In 1984, Ralph and Gert Fondell left Nome after twenty-five years to help the Arctic Broadcasting Association launch Christian radio stations in Anchorage and Bethel. But Ralph's departure left a vacuum in leadership at KICY that would take years to fill. Jim Brewer seemed the logical choice to replace Ralph as general manager. He had been involved in the ministry for four years and had been a quick study.

Under Jim's leadership KICY–FM moved from broadcasting popular instrumental music to targeting a younger audience with contemporary Christian music. The station increased its ability to provide a clear instantaneous signal by installing both a satellite dish for Associated Press feeds and a larger satellite dish for high quality network feeds at the station. But Jim's devotion to his work at times became all-consuming. In the summer of 1986 Jim stepped down as general manager. That was also the year Terry and Linda Reynolds moved to Anchorage to serve as chief engineer for the fledgling network of ABA stations. When the general manager's position became vacant, there was no way of predicting how difficult it would be to fill.

The loss of the Fondells, the Reynolds, the Summers, and the Brewers within a short time took an emotional toll on the remaining staff. At the same time, financial contributions to KICY began to plummet. Dean Dray, interim pastor at the Golovin Covenant Church, stepped in to lead KICY for six months.

With a shortage of volunteers, morale was at an all-time low. In the spring of 1987, Don Severson, a retired oil executive from Bellevue, Washington, and his wife, Carol, agreed to move up to Nome and take over as interim manager of the struggling radio ministry. With the enthusiastic involvement of Doris Ahwinona, a local Alaska Native, the Seversons' transition was eased.

Dan and Laura Smith, laypersons from a church in Gig Harbor, Washington, also proved to be a God-send. Their contribution not only

Dan Smith
(seated) and
Jim Engwall

buoyed Don and Carol but the entire operation of the station. As a trained engineer, Dan tackled critical projects, such as installing KICY's first digital automation system. Laura's ability in and around the office was indispensable to Carol.

In July 1987, Lynne Cox, a thirty-year-old long distance swimmer, arrived in Nome with an entourage. She began training off the coast of Nome in preparation for an unprecedented swim. Within a couple weeks Cox pushed off from the shoreline of Little Diomede Island in the U.S. and propelled herself in 38-degree water through the Bering Strait until she reached Big Diomede Island in the Soviet Union. The swim lasted two hours and sixteen minutes and was a remarkable athletic achievement of endurance. In a time that predated the fall of Communism, it was also a remarkable diplomatic achievement. Following her swim, Presidents Reagan and Gorbachev toasted Cox in Washington D.C., saying that she "proved by her courage how closely to each other our peoples live."

In addition, the beleaguered staff of KICY was inspired by the perseverance of one person to accomplish what had previously seemed humanly impossible. As the station provided coverage of Cox's swim for the CBS radio network as well as news stations in Seattle and San Francisco, the staff couldn't help but be motivated. Cox's achievement was also a strong reminder of how close KICY's Russian-speaking neighbors were— and, perhaps most significantly, she had cracked a door open for personal contact. Axel Karlson's goal of getting the gospel into Russia through the backdoor was within view.

Despite the staff's determination, however, storm clouds continued to hang over the station. As long as KICY struggled to pay bills and recruit self-supporting volunteers, the station's ability to sustain, let alone increase its outreach to the Soviet Far East and the eighty villages of its listening area, was questionable. Don Severson gave a much needed shot in the arm to the operation, but his inexperience in broadcasting and fundraising proved to be personally frustrating and resulted in the Seversons' return to Washington in the spring of 1988.

In 1987 John McBride was the director of Child Evangelism Fellowship in Fort Collins, Colorado. One Sunday while attending the Covenant church where he and his family were members, a notice in the bulletin caught his eye. There was a need for someone to manage the denomination's radio station in Nome, Alaska. With experience in both broadcasting and retail management, John knew he had the qualifications. Further, he and his wife, Sherrie, were open to whatever new adventures God might have for them.

John sent a letter of inquiry, but by the time Arctic Broadcasting Association learned of his interest, they had hired Don as interim manager. A year later, however, Ralph Fondell called John to ask if he was still interested in the position, and John was all the more convinced it was God's will. Within two months of Ralph's contact, in April 1988, the McBrides were unpacking their belongings in the brown house.

John
McBride

Soon after they arrived, John and Sherrie found themselves hosting a string of farewell parties for volunteers whose plans to return home had been made even before they had arrived. It didn't take long for John to realize he had half the number of staff that was required to maintain the current programming.

But a staff shortage was far from John's only challenge. There was also the funding shortage to deal with. Contributions fell while costs associated with operating the station continued to go up. The five homes that KICY owned for staff and volunteers were in need of refurbishment. On top of all that, within a few weeks of their arrival, Sherrie discovered that the tundra vegetation triggered her allergies, which then developed into asthma and an auto-immune disorder.

KICY's voyage into the future seemed destined to be a stormy one. As John was finding his footing, a political tidal wave was sweeping across the globe. The world's borders were shrinking overnight. With the collapse of the Berlin Wall on November 9, 1989, a chain reaction in international politics had begun. In Czechoslovakia Czechs and Slovaks took to the streets to demand political reforms. A month later Ceausescu's Communist regime in Romania was overthrown by popular protest. Soon, the Communist parties of Bulgaria and Albania also ceded power. The revolutions of 1989 marked the death knell of Communism in Europe. By 1991, Gorbachev was forced to cede power to Yeltsin, who oversaw the dissolution of the Soviet Union.

The McBrides arrived in Nome as contact and trade were finally being established between Alaska and the Soviet Far East. Beginning in 1988, Alaska Airlines promoted "friendship flights" between Nome and Provideniya, Chukotka. John joined the American delegation on two of these trips. There he met individuals in the region of Anadyr who acknowledged listening to KICY. John returned to Nome motivated to place an increased emphasis on Russian programming. He expanded the thirty-minute Russian programming at the end of each day to ninety minutes.

John also had a passion to reach lost people in and around Nome. Day after day as he drove from the station to the post office to retrieve the mail, he saw the same twenty to thirty people on Front Street stumbling to keep their balance as they frequented Nome's many bars. John knew many of these had grown up going to Sunday school in one of the thirteen churches in town. They'd listened to "Ranger Bill" and "Sailor Sam" on KICY as kids. But lack of meaningful employment, absentee parents, years of unthinkable harsh weather, and constant peer pressure had taken its toll. The situation in the villages was just as bleak. Unemployment, alcoholism, and drug use gave way to chronic depression, drinking related deaths, and suicide.

The findings of the 1990 census revealed that 40 percent of the Alaska Native population was under age eighteen, compared to 30 percent of the non-Native population. The average age of the Alaska Native population was 24, and the average age of non-Alaska Natives was 29.5. The suicide rate of Alaska Native teens and young adults in KICY's listening area was three times that of non-Native youth of the same age group in other parts of the country. In addition to the census findings, the station received results of a listener survey showing that KICY enjoyed a large listening audience in Nome, but only 6 percent of the people outside of Nome were listening to the station.

John challenged the staff to find a way to reach the villages, and especially the youth who desperately needed to hear the good news of the gospel. As far as John was concerned, reaching this young audience required a significant change in programming. Together, they devised a plan to reach the younger age bracket by changing from a secular country and gospel music format to a secular rock and contemporary Christian music format. In addition to appealing to younger non-Christians, the new format would attract more advertising from local merchants. The plan was presented to and approved by the ABA board.

But because the board was concerned that the station maintain its commitment to being a Christian station, it insisted that John's plan include an increase in the production and scheduling of "God Spots." The board felt that with more non-Christians listening to the station, it was essential for the station to find creative ways of referencing how much God love the world as well as what Christians believe. The new format also presented opportunities to call or write in for Christian literature.

The change in format did have some effect: "I met a man in one of the villages who had accepted Jesus as Savior because of our broadcast," John recalled. "It completely transformed the relationship with his wife and family. And when the gold fields were being worked we heard of people who were unsaved singing along with one of the contemporary Christian songs he'd learned while listening to KICY on his earphones. Amazingly a fellow miner who was a Christian heard him and used that opportunity to witness to him about the Lord."

While the ABA board was concerned with finding new ways to increase the number of listeners to KICY in the villages, they were also eager to maximize the Russian programming at night. At the ABA meetings in September 1995, Ted Haney, president of the board, proposed that the ABA apply to the FCC to increase KICY's power from the hours of 11 a.m. to 4 p.m. from 10,000 to 50,000 watts, the maximum allowed for AM stations. His proposal called for adding two additional towers to the transmitter site so the 50,000 watts of radio signal could be focused directly toward Russia.

Ted, whose passion for global outreach can be traced to his years as executive director of Far East Broadcasting Company, explained his rationale had to do with reaching as many people as possible. Given KICY's northerly latitude, it was in a unique position to accomplish what no other station could do. A directional signal powered by 50,000 watts could penetrate 2,000 miles into the Russian Far East.

Another ABA board member, Dan Johnson, was also encouraging KICY to look at increasing their Russian language ministry. Dan had worked on staff at KICY in the mid-eighties and in 1993 he was commissioned by the Covenant to be a special assignment missionary working in Magadan, Russia. (In 1996, he would launch the first Christian FM radio station in Russia.) Dan and his staff were already providing KICY with material and could provide even more if the station increased its Russian language programming.

Dan Johnson (seated) with Russian radio staff

Some members of the board felt that the estimated $385,000 price tag for the project was too great for the station. Others doubted the FCC would permit it. The board eventually agreed to take the first step and approach the FCC with the request that KICY be allowed to increase it power to 50,000 watts and go with a directional signal into Russia during the hours of 11 p.m. to 4 a.m.

A few months after the ABA submitted the application, the FCC rejected the request. For the better part of a year, attorneys in Washington, D.C. argued KICY's case on behalf of the ABA. The FCC continued to deny the request, citing the same two reasons. First, the engineers were concerned about interference with other stations in Alaska and the lower forty-eight. Second, the FCC had never received a request like this before and they were concerned about allowing such a powerful directional signal into a foreign country.

Ted and his ABA colleagues refused to give up. Even those who had initially had doubts about the proposal were determined to keep trying. The FAA in Alaska had no problems with the additional towers, as long as they were the same height as the original one. Having spent extended time in prayer, the board urged Ted, who had personal contacts at the FCC, to go back to the capital and make one last attempt at resolving the problem.

"I don't remember everything about the trip," Ted admitted, "but I do recall I didn't sleep very well the night before I met with the FCC engineers on the interference issue. I didn't know what their bottom-line objections were, and therefore I didn't know how to respond to them."

The next day, Ted worked hard to understand the engineers' concerns. By asking the right questions he realized the engineers had overlooked that the station's request was for an increase in power during the hours of 11 p.m. to 4 a.m. and for a directional signal which would be pointed west. Ted pointed out that KICY's request meant that almost all of the signal would be directed away from Alaska and the lower forty-eight and that when they were not operating with a directional signal, KICY would be broadcasting at its usual 10,000 watts. After hearing this, the FCC engineers looked at each other and one of them said, "You know, he is right. There is not an interference problem."

But this only addressed one of the FCC's concerns. Since the increased signal would be aimed toward Russia, another entity had to sign-off on the proposed action. The next step was to present the request to the International Telecommunications Union in Switzerland. They in turn required that KICY's request be published in the ITU international publication three times to allow for other nations to register a complaint. This part of the process required much more patience than waiting for the Bering Sea to thaw each spring. It lasted almost two more years.

During this waiting time, the staff's growing enthusiasm over the Super Power Project (as the new towers and wattage upgrade was called) began to cool. Some Covenanters in the villages began to write letters to John McBride dismayed that KICY wasn't the station it used to be. Many of these were listeners who didn't relate to the format directed at teens and young adults. The automated format, although it eased the grueling demands on the staff, was viewed as impersonal and fueled impressions by western Alaska Covenant churches that KICY was getting further away from its mission.

Some of the dissatisfaction with KICY also stemmed from the fact that the station and its staff were not as involved in the community in the same ways that previous staff had been. The smaller staff meant that the station could not do as much live programming, so KICY discontinued popular programming, such as the broadcasting of local basketball games. The station began relying primarily on automated pre-recorded programs and music. Further, the overworked staff did not feel that they had time to be involved in civic matters and did not serve on local boards or attend local functions as much as before. All of this combined to create an impression that KICY was being operated by "outsiders" who came to Nome to serve, but did not put the effort into getting to know people and understand their programming needs.

Some who were disenchanted with KICY complained to the ECCAK leadership council, which appointed the Arctic Broadcasting Association board. A growing chasm developed between the station management and those who lobbied for a more overtly Christian format and a more responsive staff.

As John continued to deflect negative comments about the current musical format and the actions of his staff, the morale of the KICY staff was adversely impacted. When the pastor of the Nome Covenant Church requested that the Sunday morning services no longer be carried on KICY, because of the "questionable lyrics" of secular songs played on the air, a relational hemorrhage ensued. In the words of Paul Wilson, the field director of ECCAK, the conflict was a "vision collision." The staff maintained the primary purpose of KICY was missional—to reach seekers and nonbelievers by providing a format they would listen to. Those critical of the increasingly secular format embraced a radically different philosophy of ministry. They held that KICY existed primarily for the nurture and edification of Christians.

In the midst of this growing controversy, a tragedy occurred that would rock the community. Late in the afternoon on June 27, 1997, an Olson Air Service pilot was attempting to land in Nome in dense fog. His sole passenger was a seven-year-old boy who had been visiting relatives in

Teller. As the pilot approached the airport, he failed to see the KICY tower and hit it directly. Leo Rasmussen, Nome's former mayor, was manning a fireworks stand on the beach when he heard the horrific explosion. As he turned to the east he could see the eerie sight. The 250-foot antenna and the single engine plane crashed to the ground. Both the pilot and the boy were killed.

KICY radio tower
after being hit by
an airplane

In western Alaska, travel by small plane is common and plane crashes are a part of life. Still this crash affected the community deeply. The loss of life, particularly of the young boy, coupled with the fact that the family that owned Olson Air Service was well known and respected in Nome and nearby Golovin and active in the Covenant Church made this tragedy that much more profound.

For the KICY staff the grief they felt over the loss of life coupled with their concern for the Olson family was compounded by the fact that the station had lost its AM signal. Further, not only was the tower destroyed, the transmitter was also damaged during the accident. Not only would a new tower have to be shipped to Nome, but a new transmitter would also have to be purchased and installed. For a staff that was already feeling overworked and under attack this time proved especially stressful.

For three months the AM portion of KICY's programming was off the air. This was particularly frustrating to the staff as they felt that the programming they had to offer would be meaningful to the community as they coped with the effects of the plane crash.

By the first week in October, KICY was back on the air, with a new tower and transmitter. KNOM graciously provided valuable technical and engineering assistance to KICY to speed up the process of getting KICY back on the air. The spirit of cooperation between KICY and KNOM showed an acknowledgement that both stations existed for the purpose of seeing God's kingdom furthered here on earth.

Unfortunately, the tension between KICY and the western Alaska Covenant churches resurfaced when the staff returned to the same program format. A stalemate had developed that would require the ABA board of directors to intervene. For several months board members agonized over how to resolve a situation that was negatively impacting the radio station as well as the body of Christ in the eyes of the community. Ironically, it was at this very time that the FCC cleared the way for KICY to move ahead with the Super Power Project by signing off on a construction permit for the transmitter site improvements.

At the June 1998 board meeting, ABA weighed all the evidence and concluded that the Covenant Church in Alaska would best be served by operating a radio station that was primarily targeted to the needs of growing Christians. What had been true with regard to programming in 1960 and for the first decade of the station's ministry was no longer the case. Western Alaskans now had a plethora of other sources for entertainment, news, and secular music. By attempting to compete with other broadcast media, KICY had struggled to find its niche. In addition, many of the village churches did not have full-time pastors, and Christians looked to KICY for inspiration and teaching not otherwise available. The board also felt that the KICY staff also needed to be more involved in the community and to provide more live programming, which was one need that had not changed in the thirty-eight years since the station began.

The ABA board also felt that since John McBride was more committed to radio outreach, that he would not be the best person to carry out the desired change in format. With regret, John submitted his resignation, ending a decade of long and faithful service to KICY.

Dave Oseland, a broadcast engineer at Channel 38 television in Chicago for twenty-three years (and a past owner of a Christian radio station in Missouri) had known about KICY for years. Intrigued by the station's history, mission, and adventuresome setting, he agreed to serve as interim manager for up to one year. He and Jim Persson, executive director of church growth and evangelism (formerly home mission) for the Covenant from 1990 through 1998, both attended Ravenswood Evangelical Covenant

Church in Chicago. In fact in 1997, at the height of the format wars and during a particularly difficult financial time at KICY, Jim had solicited Dave's help. The Covenant paid to have Dave go to Alaska to meet with Paul Wilson, field director for the ECCAK, and to travel to Nome to observe the station. In particular, Dave was asked to evaluate KICY and determine what changes needed to be made to address the concerns that were being raised. One of the conclusions Dave drew from his visit to Nome was the need for the station to be more responsive to its listeners and to do more live programming, especially in the morning from 6:30 to 9 a.m. He also proposed that the station start an on-air prayer and devotional program that would minister to the needs of those living in the listening area.

The problems awaiting Dave in Nome included more than just the controversy over format. Since 1997, ABA, ECCAK, and the Covenant denomination had been struggling to address a number of important issues. First and foremost was how to relieve the pressure on staff that had reached a crisis point during the format wars. Further, although appropriations had stopped in 1984, the Covenant, through the Department of Church Growth and Evangelism (formerly Department of Home Mission), had continued to stand with ABA and provided financial support, when necessary, in the form of loans. By August 1998, the loan amount had risen to over $1 million and it appeared that KICY would not be able to repay this debt. The denomination was so concerned about this issue, that in 1997 they had asked Dave, in addition to evaluating the station, to use his contacts in the religious broadcast market to determine if there were any organizations interested in buying KICY.

In 1998 the financial situation was so serious that in August the Board of Church Growth and Evangelism passed a resolution requiring the ABA to begin making at least interest payments on its loan by January 1999 or else the station would be forced to close. Other causes were being hampered by having so much capital tied up in a single operation.

Knowing all this, Dave arrived in Nome the end of August 1998. Immediately, he faced two major tasks. First, he needed to implement the board policy to phase in an all-Christian music format on the AM station. In deference to the tastes of those who had lobbied for all-Christian music, the genre of music that would now characterize KICY-AM was southern gospel music. After consulting with the remaining staff, he determined that the format change would begin October 1. Dave's second task was to explore all possible means of debt reduction, including continuing to seek a buyer for the station and its license.

The station had to replace hundreds of records and CDs. The equipment was in disrepair. The departure of the McBrides triggered other staff vacancies. Winter was approaching. Dave realized that if the station was to survive, God would need to work another miracle, just as God had done did almost forty years earlier when the station began.

Fortunately, Dave was not alone in facing these challenges. John McBride had graciously agreed to stay for a month to assist him with the transition. Mark Hill, a veteran youth worker with ECCAK's youth ministry program Covenant Youth of Alaska, agreed to come to Nome to help fill the vacancies. Mark "Swede" Hanson, grandson of Ralph Hanson, had just begun his time at the station. Amy Bancroft, who had been at the station for a year, and Frances Whitmore were the only staff who remained.

Dave Oseland
and Frances
Whitmore

Frances, a retired teacher from California, had come to Nome in 1990 to volunteer on a short-term basis with KICY. She enjoyed Nome so much that after two years she sold her California home and made Nome her permanent address. Frances worked for Alaska Airlines and volunteered her time with KICY. During the difficult transition after John left, Frances's skill as KICY's traffic director, which involved placing the commercial spots in the appropriate places and maintaining the log of regularly scheduled programs, was a God-send. Her commitment to the mission of KICY was also a testament to the younger staff that remained, that even with the sadness and hurt they felt over the McBrides and others leaving, KICY was there to serve the community first and foremost.

Understandably, the skeletal staff was overwhelmed as they looked to the approaching deadline for the format change. In answer to prayer, Dave received word that Judith Chafin, a woman from Oregon, had applied to spend several months at the station. About the same time, pioneer staffer Fred Savok called and asked if he could be put to work as a volunteer. With this additional help, the small but committed staff met its goal, and on October 1, 1998, KICY initiated an all-Christian musical and teaching format.

Dave also added some live programming. The "Breakfast Club" was created to help people begin their day on a positive note. It included music and discussion with listeners on topics of local interest. This was followed by "CareForce," a program that allowed listeners to call in prayer requests. Through these two new programs, and the other old favorites, such as "Ptarmigan Telegraph" and the "Native Hour" (the new name of the "Eskimo Hour"), KICY was again connecting directly with its listeners.

With the new format up and running, Dave was committed to tackling another necessary task. Ted Haney had found two antennas, which would be added to the transmitter site once final authorization was received. Ted had discovered that a Navy base in Virginia was deactivating several towers and was able to work with a consortium of five Christian broadcasting organizations that paid the expenses for taking them down. But until the FCC gave the green light, once the ITU had approved the proposal, the towers would sit in sections on a dry dock in Seattle. There was also the issue of $385,000 that needed to be raised to pay for the new towers, a new transmitter, site improvements, and shipping. Dave decided there was no time like the present to begin a public appeal.

In each "Call Letter," progress to the enormously large goal was reported. Monies flowed in. The opportunity to penetrate so far into the former Soviet Union with an enhanced signal and directional focus motivated generosity. By June 1999, more than $265,000 had been raised.

That same month, Dave left KICY after providing invaluable leadership for the station during his time as interim manager. Just as he was leaving, KICY's old friend Bill Hartman was arriving to supervise the installation of the two additional towers at the transmitter site. Over the winter months, the FCC had indicated that formal authorization would most likely be forthcoming. That was all the encouragement Bill and the ABA board needed to ship the antennas from Seattle and arrange for their construction in the summer. With a crew of volunteers from Washington, California, Arizona, and Indiana, the sections sent by barge from Seattle were cleaned, painted, and assembled. By November the transmitter site now had two new transmission towers.

Further evidence that God was not through with KICY, was that no buyer had stepped forward and the station had found a way to make interest payments on its loan to the Covenant. Still, even after weathering another storm, KICY still had challenges to face. The station had to raise more funds and devise creative Russian programming. The new general manager who would soon arrive would be instrumental in addressing both areas.

CHAPTER TEN

Russia at Last

At 1:30 in the morning on March 13, 2003, with the wind chill way below zero, hundreds of people lined both sides of the Nome's main thoroughfare. For this little town, this major sporting event represented a turnaround of enormous proportions. The Alaska gold rush put Nome on the map in 1901. But within a few years a boom city of 20,000 was reduced to a stable population of 3,500. For much of the twentieth century Nome struggled to find an identity. Although gold mining provided a certain number of jobs, a commodity controlled by a fluctuating price could not support a steady work force. Nome struggled with a depressed economy and unemployed people in depression. But with the establishment of the Iditarod in 1973 Nome looked to tourism to help revitalize its economy.

As tourism continues to grow, Nome's economic hopes are promising. The burled arch that is wheeled on to Front Street each March to mark the finish line does more than identify the end of the Iditarod Trail. It also signals the gateway to Nome's prosperous future.

With the change in format to an all-Christian music programming, and a revitalized commitment to Russian broadcast-
ing, KICY quickly found a new identity. And with the change it had recap-
tured the excitement and momentum that first marked the radio ministry as they went on the air Easter Sunday 1960.

Leaders at the denominational offices in Chicago and Dave Oseland
in Nome had advertised the vacant position of general manager from
August 1998 to January 1999 without any serious responses. In February
1999 Paul Wilson, the field director of ECCAK, was in Chicago attending the annual Covenant ministers' Midwinter Conference. During a
break in the conference, a North Park seminary student walked up to him.
John Madvig had been a volunteer at KICY several years before and recognized the Alaska church leader. Paul told John about KICY's tenuous
situation and about the frustration related to the search for a new station
manager. As the two talked, John thought of a man in the Covenant church
in Kalamazoo, Michigan, where he had served as a youth pastor prior to
starting seminary. The man owned his own business and a recording studio. In addition, he was involved in radio production and jingle writing.
"You really need to talk to Dennis Weidler," John urged.

Willing to check out all leads, Paul called Dennis the next day and suggested he talk to Rob Hall, who worked in the Department of Church
Growth and Evangelism and was the Covenant's representative to the
ABA board. Although he was not all that interested in interrupting a successful career and moving a long way away from aging parents, Dennis
reluctantly agreed to drive the two hours to Chicago to find out more.
Weidler was not unaware of the station. In the early nineties he had submitted an application for the program direction position that was open
at that time, but he was not sure he would actually be able to give up his
business and move to Nome if the job was offered to him so he did not
pursue it any further.

What Jim Persson, executive director of church growth and evangelism, and Rob Hall shared with Weidler during his visit to Chicago was
anything but promising. The Covenant had been seeking a buyer for the
station and KICY had a huge debt and a limited staff. It had recently been
the object of divisive quarrels between Christians and churches in its

primary listening area. Even with a new general manager it was possible that if the station could not find a way to satisfy its debt, it would have to be shut down.

Having painted a realistic backdrop, Jim and Rob nonetheless encouraged Dennis to think about accepting the challenge. Instead of asking for an immediate answer, they offered to fly Dennis and his wife, Candace, to Nome to take a look at the situation for themselves. Dennis politely smiled and said they would make it a matter of prayer, but he had serious doubts about looking at the position any further.

Dennis and Candace Weidler

After discussing it among themselves, Dennis and Candace decided to accept the trip to Alaska. In May, they flew to Nome to see the station, meet the staff, and acquaint themselves with the remote community. As they slogged around town in the constant drizzle, thawing ice, and ever-present mud, they saw the legendary gold rush town at the worst time of the year. Dave Oseland, whose eleven months of interim leadership was coming to a close, did his best to coax them to take the reigns. He knew the problems associated with the station in recent years, but he had become convinced that this was a ministry with unimagined potential.

"In all honesty, I was intrigued by what I saw, but didn't think it was the right place for us," Dennis later admitted. "Unless you've been to Nome, you probably won't understand how far away from the rest of civilization it feels. After four days, Candace and I boarded our Alaska Airlines flight. I was quite sure we wouldn't be back."

But when the Weidlers returned to Michigan, they were amazed to discover that their hearts were still in Nome. There was something about that little town and the struggling station they couldn't put behind them.

Without logical explanation, they found themselves longing to return. Within a month, Dennis called Jim Persson to tell him he was willing and ready to accept the job of general manager. Putting their business up for sale, the couple began to pack, convinced that God was calling them to ministry in Nome.

When in August 1999 their plane broke through the clouds in its approach to the Nome airport, Dennis and Candace looked out the window of the Boeing 737 for a view of their new home. Instead of the one antenna they had seen from their initial visit in May, there were now the beginnings of two additional towers on the south edge of town.

Dennis hit the ground running—there was much to be done. The station was understaffed and overbudget. In the month before he arrived, KICY spent $10,000 more than it took in. Dennis also realized he had to address some relational issues. The ABA board had made the decision that with finances being so tight, Weidler would be the only paid staff position. This meant that he needed to create a team out of the individual volunteers who were working hard to hold things together. He also recognized that the station had to reestablish the strong community relationship that had marked KICY's earliest days.

Soon after the Weidlers arrived, Nome was preparing to hold its annual Labor Day Bath Tub Race. Each year, the town gathers to watch teams made up of local merchants and organizations compete to see who can push a bathtub racer down Nome's Front Street the fastest. Each tub is powered by a team of five—four pushers and one bather-driver. Dennis had a brainstorm. He entered the station in the event. Involving the staff in the annual race would address both items on his get-acquainted agen-

KICY staff and their bathtub racer

da. The staff would discover his openness to having fun and the community would meet the new station manager in town—with a microphone in one hand and a back scrubber in his other. The KICY tub came in last, but Dennis was on his way to building a team, and he certainly had introduced himself to the community.

In the September 1999 "Call Letter," the station's longtime supporters had a chance to witness Dennis's enthusiasm, as he wrote: "There are many ambitious long-term goals at KICY including the power increase to 50,000 watts, expanded Russian language programming, increased visibility in the village we serve through western Alaska and partnering with their pastors and mission staff.... Thanks for being part of our ministry in Alaska. Prayer works. We'd appreciate yours!"

Within a month, Dennis's assertive style of leadership was evident. He had built bridges with Alaska Leadership College, a lay institute for Alaska Natives that was sponsored by ECCAK, by inviting students to spend two weeks at KICY learning the operation of a radio station. Dennis also attempted to breathe new life into Arctic Ambassadors, a fundraising sponsorship club, in which those who donate money for an hour of broadcasting are publicly recognized on the air. Although the club had been around for a while, no one had had time to put much effort into it in the previous five years. After two months, Dennis and Candace flew to the lower forty-eight to increase the base of contributors. By his third newsletter he was able to announce that the Tower Power project was within $100,000 of its goal of $385,000.

By his third month Dennis had reintroduced listeners in Nome to live remote broadcasts from local churches and the local prison. Not to overlook the villages, he planned listener appreciation dinners for Golovin and Unalakleet, at which the staff cooked and served a meal for all those who could make it from the surrounding villages.

Although Dave Oseland had achieved the transition from secular to Christian music on the AM band, a similar transition was still needed for KICY–FM. Dennis set the deadline for the new FM format to coincide with the annual meeting of ECCAK in March. The meeting was to be held in Nome, and pastors and lay leaders from all the Covenant churches in Alaska would be attending. Weeks after the meeting the station would be observing its fortieth anniversary. Dennis recognized this as a time to celebrate, and he ordered sweatshirts, t-shirts, and note cards to mark the event.

Within the first six months of taking over, Dennis had found his stride. The enthusiasm he brought inspired those who looked to him for leadership. The young staffers were motivated by his vision. Older volunteers like Frances Whitmore and Fred Savok agreed that Dennis was God's man for this season in the life KICY.

Patty Burchell was a young volunteer whose arrival in Nome coincided with the Weidlers'. An elementary school teacher from California, she was looking for a change of pace. Seeking an adventure, she arrived in Nome ready to commit one year to working with KICY. But she soon realized that one year was not enough. She enjoyed not only hosting the "Breakfast Club," but all the things that made living in Nome fun, bonfires on the beach, picking wild Arctic berries, hiking on the tundra. Patty also made a point of getting out and meeting people, helping to re-establish the personal contact that once characterized the staff of KICY. With Dennis at the helm and volunteers on board like Patty, things were beginning to turn around.

In April 2000 as the station entered into its fifth decade of ministry, it continued to make tracks toward the future. The Tower Power project met its goal. Mark Hill, the CYAK worker who had come to KICY to help out after John McBride left, developed a new contemporary music program called "The Edge." This new live two-hour show debuted on KICY–FM and was aimed at teens and young adults in Nome. Unlike any programming attempted before, the edgy alternative music, which featured solid biblical teaching, drew new listeners.

It was also in April that Dennis proudly announced the completion of a recording studio in the basement of the station. Having disassembled his private studio in Michigan, Dennis had arranged for the components to be shipped to Nome where he donated them to KICY. The Genesis Studios featured a control room and a sound lock, a 32-input mixing console, 8-track analog, and 16-track digital recording decks, as well as a CD recorder.

Dennis envisioned using the new studio to train broadcasting students and station volunteers. Genesis Studios also improved the overall quality of Native language recordings. In addition it provided additional income to the station when outside groups wanted professional recording services. To initiate the equipment, Harvey Fiskeaux, pastor of Nome Covenant Church, recorded the studio's premier album. The collection of gospel songs, in which Harvey sang the lead and backup vocals as well as laid down the various instrumental tracks, was used as a fundraising gift.

In the summer of 2000, a tireless Bill Hartman returned for a two-month stay to supervise the completion of the project begun the previous summer. Although the new towers had been erected, construction on a new transmitter building was delayed due to a late break-up of ice on the Bering Sea the previous spring.

Genesis
Studios

Bill's contributions to KICY and the work in Alaska had been many since his first visit to Nome forty-five years earlier. In addition to laying the groundwork for the radio project in the first place, and helping with the technical aspect of KICY, he had been a tireless fundraiser, and for a number of years he oversaw the printing and mailing of the KICY "Call Letter." The Hartman Proposal passed by the 1985 Covenant Annual Meeting was a huge benefit to KICY as well as a number of other Covenant ministries. Bill also served on the ABA board for more than thirty-five years, much of that time as its secretary and treasurer. As treasurer he was always concerned that the money that people entrusted to KICY was used wisely. At one ABA board meeting in Nome in the early nineties, John McBride mentioned that the lights on the antenna tower had to be replaced. He reported that the last time the station had hired someone to do that job it had cost KICY $3,000 for the labor. As treasurer, Bill knew the station didn't have the money. So after the meeting, without telling anyone, Bill walked to the outskirts of town, climbed the 250-foot tower, and replaced the lights himself.

In April 2001, a dream that began in the heart of Ted Haney and the ABA board members six years earlier was fulfilled. The FCC notified Dennis that KICY had authority to begin broadcasting into Russia. This new license allowed KICY to multiply its power by five. At night a 50,000-watt directional signal would be beamed toward Siberia, finally realizing Axel Karlson's dream of the Covenant finding a back door to Russia.

On Sunday afternoon, June 9, 2001, a service of dedication was held at the transmitter site for the two new transmission towers. In 1958 Art Zlystra and Ralph Fondell had staked a claim to this oddly shaped plot of land that was bigger than they had needed. Now, more than forty years later, the site perfectly accommodated the three aligned towers of webbed steel.

The guest of honor that day was Bill Hartman. In recognition for his boundless enthusiasm and tireless commitment to KICY, the ABA board recommended that the new transmitter site be named for Bill Hartman and his late wife, Arlene, who had died three years earlier from cancer. Standing next to Bill as Gary Walter, executive minister of church growth and evangelism, presented him with a plaque acknowledging his contributions, was his daughter, Gail. From the time she was fourteen, she had heard about Nome and the Norton Sound but had never had the opportunity to visit the place that was so special to her father.

Margaret "Sister" Olson, vice-chairperson of the ABA board, best summed up the board's feelings: "We honor Bill because he first honored God."

Bill Hartman and his daughter, Gail, at the dedication of the Bill and Arlene Hartman transmitter site

Survey of KICY transmitter site showing three broadcast towers

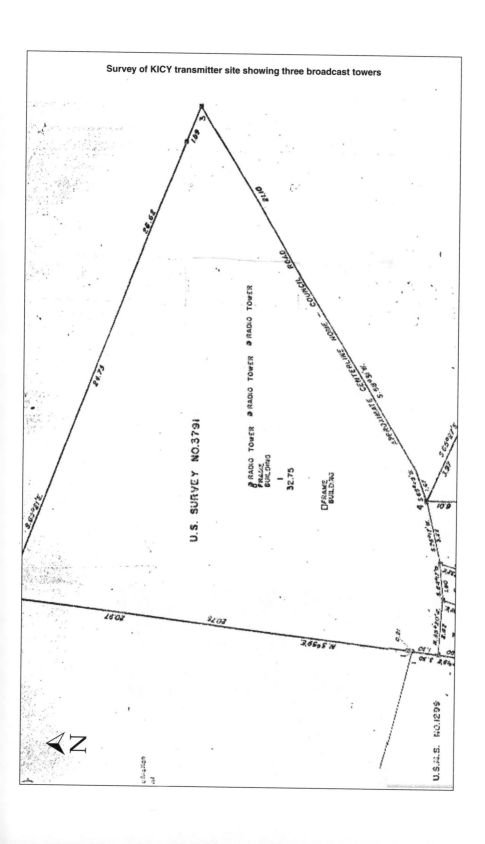

In his remarks, Bill said he was most pleased that the station would now be able to reach so much of Russia: "If when I get [to heaven]...I meet a few Russians that say, 'You know, we wouldn't be here save for KICY,' that will be enough."

Addressing the gathered crowd, Harvey Fiskeaux witnessed to the power of Christian radio. Just three days before his grandfather died, he became a Christian after listening to a sermon on the radio.

"God's word is the power behind the tower, and God's word is going to do the work," he said. "The people of western Alaska and Russia need someone to tell the story. The greatest miracle is a changed heart for a man or a woman who is lost."

With the towers up and running the station was now prepared to expand its ministry to Russia, but it needed more than additional broadcasting power. KICY needed staff to direct the expanded programming.

Ellen and Andrei Sarazov were attending a church in Kansas City when they were approached by someone who had read in the "Call Letter" that KICY was looking for Russian-speaking volunteers. The Sarazovs had recently returned from the central Asian republic of Kyrgyzstan, where Ellen had served as a missionary. There she had met Andrei, and they had recently married. Following the 9/11 terrorist attacks, Americans had been encouraged to leave Kyrgyzstan, so Ellen and Andrei had moved to the U.S.

In July 2002, three months after first hearing about KICY, Ellen and Andrei arrived in Nome and settled into the yellow house next door to the studio building. As many had done before them, the Sarazovs found employment in the community, while donating their time to KICY.

Ellen and Andrei Sarazov

Within a few days of their arrival, Andrei was producing a half-hour Russian language news program, focusing on Christianity in the world. This program was aired each night along with additional programming received from Dan Johnson, who by now had started New Life Radio, a Christian satellite network in Russia. From 11 p.m. to 4 a.m. each night, KICY was able to touch the lives of those living on the Chukotkan peninsula 150 miles due west of Nome, with programs that included regional news, weather, and inspirational programming.

Chukotkan Pastors and Lay Leaders Conference at the Presbyterian Church in Gambell

Before that summer was over, the Sarazovs flew to the village of Gambell on St. Lawrence Island. There they met with a group of Siberian Yupik pastors and lay people from Russia who annually convene with Siberian Yupik church leaders from Alaska for a week of fellowship, worship, and teaching. Andrei and Ellen were thrilled to hear how listeners beyond the Bering Sea have benefited from the broadcasts of KICY for years.

In 2003 Dennis Weidler was elected president of the Nome Rotary Club, served as a member of the Nome Chamber of Commerce, as well as the Nome Ministerial Association. Because of the essential role aviation plays in rural Alaska, Dennis has sought to build relationships with local bush airlines and is a board member of the Christian Pilots Association. In addition, he has provided audio services for the City of Nome and Nome Public Schools and has proudly served on the Iditarod Trail Committee.

"I stress to our staff that our radio work is vital to our listeners," Dennis wrote to a KICY supporter. "But the fact that we are a Christian radio station demands that we do more than that. In essence, what we do in our community is the real reflection of our Christian faith. Our involvement validates the music we play and the messages we broadcast."

With a renewed sense of purpose and a clearly defined format, KICY is now well positioned for ministry in the coming years. In 1999, thanks to a generous commitment by the Department of Church Growth and Evangelism, KICY's debt, which was in excess of one million dollars, was reduced to $600,000. Thanks to consistent and innovative fundraising by a marketing-minded manager and a number of sizable bequests, KICY was able to fully pay off the entire $600,000 debt in just four years and nine months. At the November 2003 ABA board meeting the mortgage was burned as the board sang praises to God. Now as the station approaches its fiftieth anniversary, it is entirely debt-free.

ABA is also committed to being fiscally responsible with the resources that God has entrusted to it, and for that reason it has decided that the general manager will be the only paid staff position. All other functions at the station are done by volunteers, some who come from Nome and others who come from the lower forty-eight for periods of one to three years and raise their own support. The installation of state-of-art technology makes it easier to operate the station, leaving more time for the staff to travel to meet with listeners, and to do more live programming, as well as be more active in community affairs.

Despite the advent of cell phones, computers, snow machines, and satellite TV dishes, radio continues to be the best way to reach the people who live within the immediate broadcast area of KICY. This is proven by the continued popularity of the "Ptarmigan Telegraph," which is aired six times a day on KICY. And through it all KICY remains committed to

In November 2003 the Arctic Broadcasting Association board of directors burned KICY's mortgage.

providing a positive, informative, edifying Christian message, and continues to look for opportunities to expand its ministry to reach more people.

In 2003 KICY seized upon such an opportunity. In the early part of
that year, radio station KABN in Anchorage went off the air. It had been
the only station in the state that would have been affected by KICY if it
broadcast at 50,000 watts for twenty-four hours a day rather than just
11 p.m. to 4 a.m. KICY applied to the FCC with a request to increase its
power for those additional nineteen hours, and in December 2003, the
FCC granted the station's request. KICY's potential audience in Alaska
increased from approximately 40,000 to 600,000, plus some additional
potential listeners in Canada.

New studio
and equipment
at KICY

Dennis Weidler is ready to take advantage of this wonderful opportunity. "Because our infrastructure has been completely rebuilt, we are in a
position to focus on content," he observed. "My goal is to have our listeners feel their day isn't complete without listening to KICY. I want them
to tune in so not to risk missing something important in our broadcast
that could touch their life for good."

This focus on content includes expanding KICY's Russian language
programming. In March 2004, KICY was able to launch a Russian language "CareForce" prayer request program with Larissa Pokhilko of
Provideniya, Russia, serving as host. KICY hopes eventually to serve the
needs of its listeners in the Russian Far East by having a Russian-language
version of "Ptarmigan Telegraph."

Up in heaven, Axel Karlson is smiling.

KICY General Managers

KICY Volunteers

Every effort has been made to include the names of all the individuals who have volunteered their time and efforts at KICY. Arctic Broadcasting Association apologizes if there are any omissions, and will gladly make corrections to any future printings.

Elsie Ahlem
Doris Ahwinona
Eric Allen
Jim Allen
H. Roald Amundsen
Harriet Amundsen
Alvin Anderson
Ann-Helen Anderson
Dean Anderson
Doneetsa Anderson
Janet Anderson
Kathleen Anderson
Katy Anderson
Lois Anderson

Pam Anderson
Patricia Anderson
Sherwood W. Anderson
Alan Anway
Irene Anway
Dave Archibald
Irene Armstrong
Greg Asimakoupoulos
Wendy Asimakoupoulos
Karen Asp
Mark Aswege
Morgan Aukongak
Dan Bachelder
Everett Bachelder

Joel Bachelder
Mina Bachelder
Amelia Bafus
Duane Bailey
Sally Bailey
Brenda Baker
Dewey Bakken
Lillian Bakken
Amy Bancroft
Charlotte Baversjo
Bill Bentler
Dorothy Bentler
Craig Bergstrom
Ken Bjorlin

Marv Bjorlin
Peter Bjorlin
Karl Blatter
Eloise Bowen
Greg Bowman
Bill Bowser
Catherine Brent
Dorothy Brewer
James Brewer
Steven J. Brockman
Karen Bronczyk
Stanley Bronczyk
Doug Brown
Jack Brown
Byron Bruckner
Donald Bruckner
Eunice Bruckner
Sue Bruckner
John Brunn
Malinee Brunn
David Brush
Patty Burchell
Jerry Bush
William Byrd
Cheryl Cameron
Mary Ann Capps
Barbara Carlson
Carolee Carlson
Dave Carlson
David Carlson
Elizabeth Carlson
Elly Carlson
Gordon Carlson
Jim Carlson
Joel Carlson
Josh Carlson
Laurel Carlson
Marie Carlson

Myron Carlson
Paul Carlson
Paul B. F. Carlson
Sharon Carlson
Sharon M. Carlson
Timothy Carlson
Wayne Carlson
Jim Carrington
Victoria Carter
Russell Cervin
Judith Chafin
Bill Chipman
Scott Christiansen
David Cochran
Jim Congdon
Myron Cooter
Doreen Corwin
Dan Coy
Doug Crabb
Jeanne Crabb
Traci Craig
Nolan Cramer
James Crappuchettes
Norman Crider
Bjorlin Curtis
Jeff Curtis
Richard Dahlberg
Mary J. Damson
Steve Damson
Margaret Davidson
Elaine Daw
Roy Daw
Winfield Dean
William Deanna
Buck Delkettie
Chris Dembroski
Debbie Dennis
Dave DeVries

Kathy DeVries
Dan Dietrich
Marvin Donkers
Walt Dotomain
Karen Dunstan
Scott Dwyer
Josh Eichorn
Al Ekland
John Engstrom
Peter Engstrom
James Engwall
Marv Eppard
Janice Eppard
Jan M. Epps
Donna Erickson
Jeff Erickson
Jon Erickson
Kathy Erickson
Kris Erickson
Dr. J. Erling
Karen Fagerstrom
Art Falk
Lee Fiske
Harvey Fiskeaux
John Florance
Sue Fog
Albin Folden
Daniel Fondell
Gert Fondell
Norman Fox
Matula Frank
Carole Franklin
Alice Fredrickson
J. Erling Fredrickson
Keith Fullerton
Kaci Fullwood
Brad Gavin
Kelly Gavin

Ned Gavin	Linda Hedin	Catherine Jung
Keith Gerdin	Howard Heikes	Lou Keipers
Craig Gilbert	Kurt Helgerson	Teddy Keipers
Angie Glandien	James Hendershot	Helen Kimoktoak
Elia Gomez	Hervel Hensley	Brenda Kipp
Janet Gomez	JoAnna Hill	Gary Klodt
Deborah Grace	Mark Hill	Kay Knodel
Gary Greenland	Chip Hipkins	Henry Kohl
Garcia Guadalupe	John Hjelm	Alfred Krinke
Dolores Guilliam	Jeff Hoglund	Kim Krinke
Tom Guilliam	Sue Holder	Dale Kroeker
Bob Gunther	Tim Holder	Donna Kroeker
Dennis Gustafson	Karin Holmberg	Jerry Kroeker
Jack Gwaltney	Bill Hubbard	Karen J. Kroeker
Wayne Haas	Brenda Huidirig	Kenneth J Kroeker
Kari Hahn	Jim Hulse	Steven J. Kroeker
Evie Haight	Andy Hultgren	Franz Kugelman
Janet Hallman	Charles Hunter	Phillip Kugzruk
Newt Hallman	Ken Hviding	Louis Kuipers
Janet Hallstan	Clarence Irrigoo	Linda Kussman
Kate Hamilton	Bill James	Todd Kussman
Kathleen Hamilton	Millie James	Colene Lange
Ingeborg Handeland	Duane Janssen	Tom LaPaze
John Handeland	Marina Jarvis	Art Larson
Ted Haney	Thomas Jarvis	David Larson
Mary Hansen	Carl Johnson	Deb Larson
David Hanson	Dan Johnson	George Larson
Janet Hanson	Deanna Johnson	Hazel Larson
Mark Hanson	Don Johnson	Jim Larson
Ralph Hanson	Jeff Johnson	Linda Larson
Julie Hardley	Kirk Johnson	Robert C. Larson
Alvin Harms	Laura Johnson	Susan Larson
Jeff Harris	Peter Johnson	Diane Lawton
Barbara Harshberger	Richard Johnson	Jay Lawton
Gerald Harshberger	Steve Johnson	George Lazelle III
Wayne Harter	Tom Johnson	Mike Leander
Bill Hartman	Will Johnson	Bob Lee
Kathy Hayden	Robert Jones	Erik Lex

Emory Lindgren	Judy McMurtry	Walter Outwater
Betty Lindholm	Gordon Mesdahl	Glenda Paniptchuk
Karen Lindholm	Gordy Mesedahl	Kris Patch
Paul Lindholm	Kristen Mesdahl	Kerm Paulson
Stan Lindskoog	Jeremy Miller	Dan Pearson
Bruce Linscheid	Tim Miller	Henry Pearson
Sue Linscheid	Edna Mitchell	Chris Perrigo
Susan Linscheid	Martin Mitchell	Ron Persson
Hal Lloyd	Kevin Mobley	Chad Peterson
Ruby Lodien	Greg Mohr	Deb Peterson
Verne Lodien	Dana Moon	Janice Peterson
Christy Loux	Byron Moses	Sheldon Peterson
Steve Loux	Terry Mullenbach	Verle G. Peterson
Judy Lukjan	Chester Mute	Bryan Pickett
Dick Lundberg	Tom Mute	Chris Pillar
Mike Lundeen	Chris Nagaruk	June Polo (Harrison)
Nancy Lundeen	Marelle Nagle	Lyle Polson
Marilyn MacCrackin	Richard Nagle	Gerald Pomeroy
Dick Mack	Alyona Natwick	Beth Pond
Dorothy Mack	Carl Nelson	Janet Potomain
John Madvig	Dick Nelson	Donna Powell
Paul Madvig	Jane Nelson	William E. Powell
Tina Madvig	Howie Nelson	Carol Qualman
Lisa Magnuson	Margaret Nelson	Daniel Qualman
Dan Malone	Pat Nelson	David Rapp
Betty Mankell	Steve Nelson	Greg Ratzlaff
Judy Mankell	William Nelson	Laura Rawalt
Sherman Mankell	Lillian Ness	Edna Razzler
Edna Marfori	Myron Ness	Marcus Reese
David Martin	Scott Nichols	Scott Reeve
Debbie Martin	Sarah Njaa	Alan Reynolds
Marty Matoon	Ruth Noratuk	Linda Reynolds
Lowell Matson	Chuck Nowell	Terry Reynolds
Nancy Mattson	Diana O'Keefe	David Ries
Frank Matula	John Olfelt	Diane Riley
Kathy McBride	Margaret Olson	Holly Rockwell
David McBride	Rebecca Olson	Richard Rogers
Sherri McBride	David Oseland	Bill Romanelli

Wayne Rosenquist
Blanche Rosin
Irvin Rottrup
Brad Rud
Laura Rud
Sandra Rylatt
Palmer Sagoonick
Ted Sagoonick
Deb Sandberg
Mike Savage
Fred Savok
Gladys Savok
Elmer Sawatzky
Mark Schibilla
Dave Schmer
Christian Schweizer
Mary Schweizer
Charles Sebastian
Lois Seestrom
Carol Severson
Erika Severson
Peter Sheff
David C. Shinen
Mitzi Shinen
Deb Shold
Mike Shreeve
Bob Sieberg
Jeff Siemers
Yvonne Sievert
Scott Simonsen
Ludwig Siqueland
Paul Sjoholm
Bill Skinner
Allyson Skoien
David Sladkey
Linda Sladkey
April Smelzer
Mel Smelser

Steve Smit
Daniel Smith
Laura Smith
Rebecca Smith
Kelly Smyth
Serguei Sossedkine
Mark Spann
Dave Spear
Paul Stayboldt
Jean Stewart
Josie Stiles
Bryan Storm
Connie Strachan
Ed Strachan
Arlene Strand
Spencer Strand
Barbara Strom
Jason Stromstad
Beth Summers
Jennifer Summers
Peter Summers
Stan Summers
Kori Sump
June Sundeen
Ivan L. Sundstrom
Lloyd Sundstrom
Vesta Sundstrom
Karen Sunquist
Scott Swanberg
Annabelle Swanson
Bernie Swanson
Chip Swanson
David Swanson
Doug Swanson
Joanne Swanson
Lynn Swanson
Karl Swensen
Deb Swenson

Waldon Swenson
Charles Swoboda
Brad Syverson
Charlene Taniguchi
Tim Tattan
Brent Taylor
Dave Taylor
Hank Thimsen
Alyce Thomas
Gary Thomas
L.D. Thomas
Peter Thorpe
Amy Tisdale
Eugene Totten
Marilou Totten
Mike Totten
Jim Towner
Bill Trice
Larry Trice
Cheryl Tufts
Fred Tugge
Warren Udd
Barbara Ungar
William Updegrove
Bernice Vlahakos
Sidney Wade
Candace Weidler
Bruckner Wendell
Kathy Wenell
Kelly Whalen
Mark Whitehead
Laura Whitehouse
Frances Whitmore
James Widboom
Jeffrey Wiebe
Ken Wilder
Natalie Wilds
Sarah Wilson

Glen Wolf
Charlotte Wolfe
Barb Wood
Geoffrey P. Woodberry
Gary Woods
Robert Wooley

Teresa Woolsey
Daniel Yorkston
Don Yorkston
James Yorkston
Laurel Young
Tom Young

Allen Zellmer
Pearl Zellmer
Carl W. Ziegler
Margaret Zylstra

SOURCES

Almquist, L. Arden. *Covenant Missions in Alaska*. Chicago: Covenant Press, 1962.

"Covenant to Build Radio Station." In *Covenant Weekly*. (November 15, 1957): 1-2.

Hartman, Bill. "Shorts Stories." Unpublished manuscript.

Lindgren, Emory. *Northern Alaska in the 40's*. Self-published, 1999.

Lindholm, Paul. "KICY Celebrating Twenty-five Years This Month." In *The Covenant Companion* 74, no. 4 (April 1985): 20-24.

Lindholm, Paul. "The Voice of the Arctic." Unpublished manuscript, 1986.

Nome Nugget (March 28, 1960, April 15, 1960).

Olsson, Karl. *By One Spirit*. Chicago: Covenant Press, 1962.

Schroder, Jan-Olov. "Grandpa." translated by Sigurd F. Westberg. Unpublished essay.

"A Strong Tower in the North." In *The Sunday School Times and Christian Herald*, (December 1978).

Zylstra, Art. "The Voice of the Arctic." In *Our Covenant 1961*. Chicago: Covenant Press, 1961.

PHOTO CREDITS

Pages 4, 39-40, 42, 54-57, 61-62, 66, 68, 71, 73, 75, 79-84, 86-87, 92-94, 99, 101, 103, 110, 112, 118 courtesy of Ralph Fondell

Pages 11-13, 19-20, 22-24, 28, 30, 46 courtesy of Covenant Archives and Historical Library, located at North Park University, Chicago, Illinois

Pages 14, 131, 137 courtesy of Rob Hall

Pages 25, 29 courtesy of Covenant Communications

Pages 31, 70 courtesy of Department of the Ordered Ministry

Page 45 courtesy of Department of World Mission

Page 97 courtesy of Winfield Dean

Pages 115, 121, 127-128, 134-136 courtesy of KICY

Page 121 courtesy of Dave Oseland

Page 132 courtesy of Bob Smietana

The Voice of the Arctic

KICY

AM 850 & ICY 100.3 FM

KICY is the Evangelical Covenant Church's mission radio station serving all of western Alaska and the Russian Far East. Since 1960, KICY has been a daily Christian companion for thousands of Alaskans and Russians.

The involvement of individuals and churches in the ministry of KICY is vital if we are to continue to spread the gospel and be an encouragement to believers in western Alaska and the Russian Far East. Find out how you can support the work of KICY through:

- volunteering at the station,
- serving on a work team,
- hosting a fund-raising dinner,
- pledging financial support.

For more information, call 800-478-5429 or visit the KICY website.

WWW.KICY.ORG

R I E M U Ñ O Z

Celebrated and revered Alaskan artist RIE MUÑOZ, supplied the cover art for *Ptarmigan Telegraph—The Story of Radio Station KICY* from her 1976 image "Ptarmigan Telegraph" (Rie Muñoz Ltd., 1976). Rie (from Marie) began painting Alaskan scenes soon after arriving in the capital city of Juneau in 1951. During her years in Alaska, Muñoz has lived in a variety of small Alaskan communities, including prospecting and mining camps. Her unique watercolor paintings reflect an interest in the day-to-day activities of Alaska village life such as fishing, berry picking, children at play, as well as her love of folklore and legends.

RIE MUÑOZ's art is available in more than 150 galleries and shops. Those interested in learning more about Rie and her art work are encouraged to visit her website.

W W W . R I E M U N O Z . C O M